Space Girl Dead on Spaghetti Junction

An Anthology of Writings by
Nick Redfern

Typeset by Jonathan Downes,
Edited and Proofread by Simon Reames
Cover and Layout by SPiderKaT for CFZ Communications
Using Microsoft Word 2000, Microsoft , Publisher 2000, Adobe Photoshop CS.

First published in Great Britain by CFZ Press

**CFZ Press
Myrtle Cottage
Woolsery
Bideford
North Devon
EX39 5QR**

© CFZ MMXI

All rights reserved. Without limiting the rights under copyright reserved above, no part of this publication may be reproduced, stored in or introduced into a retrieval system, or transmitted, in any form of by any means (electronic, mechanical, photocopying, recording or otherwise), without the prior written permission of both the copyright owners and the publishers of this book.

ISBN: 978-1-905723-67-6

'There's a space girl dead on Spaghetti Junction.
She used to be mine, now I just can't function,'

Leader of the Alien Pack, by the *Poor Little Jimmy's*

CONTENTS

- 7. Introduction
- 13. Zero-Hour: 1982/1983
- 15. Saucer Files Exposed: 1986
- 17. Fatherly Words: 1987
- 21. The Beckenham Ball of Light: 1990
- 23. MJ12: The FBI Connection: 1993
- 27. Unexplained Ground Marking and UFO Incident: 1995
- 31. UFOs over Staffordshire: 1996
- 35. The Rising of the Moon: 1997
- 39. A Close Encounter of the Literary Kind: 1997
- 45. The Secret Life of Errol Flynn: 1998
- 51. Unconventional Aircraft: 1998
- 61. Banned - The BBC and the Bomb: 1999
- 67. Another Gig, Another Planet: 1999/2000
- 75. Foot & Mouth - Conspiracy or Accident? 2000
- 83. The C-Files, 2000/2001
- 89. Satellites from the Skies: 2001
- 95. Mystery on the Mountain: 2001
- 99. Something for the Weekend: 2001
- 103. Mothman Lives: 2002
- 105. A Conference, a Camera, a Conspiracy: 2003
- 115. In Search of the Chupacabras - New Revelations: 2005
- 121. Enter the Dragon Hunter: 2005
- 127. At the Edge: 2006
- 131. Opening the Government's X-Archive: 2006
- 139. The Strange Saga of the Hexham Heads: 2006
- 143. Happy Anniversary, Roswell UFO: 2007
- 149. Weirdness in the Woods: 2007

155. Did Aliens Invade Britain 50 Years Ago?: 2007
159. MJ12, UFOs and the FBI: 2007
161. Island of Paradise: 2008
165. An Alien Who's Who: 2008
167. The Missing Chapter: 2008
177. Manipulating the Crashed UFO Scene: 2009
185. Conferences and Cultural Clashes: 2010
187. Contactees and the Absurdities of Ufology: 2010
193. Why Roswell Will Never Be Solved: 2010
199. The Strange Tale of the Cardiff Giant: 2010
202. Afterword

Introduction

As I sit and type these words, late at night and on the fringes of Dallas, Texas, it's very hard to believe that I have now been involved in the field of writing for 28 years. Indeed, there was a time when I didn't even think I would reach my 28th year!

Back in the summer of 1979, as a 14-year-old, spiky-haired, West Midlands lout obsessed with punk-rock and new-wave music – yes I really *did* have spiky-hair back then – I had this romantic vision of me going out in-style before my teens were over, and in a fashion akin to that of Sid Vicious, of *Sex Pistols* infamy. The punk legend had shuffled off this mortal-coil only several months earlier, amid a violent haze of heroin, bloodied-needles, an over-the-hill stripper, knives, razor-blades and murder-charges.

But, the realization soon hit me that there was nothing romantic about Sid, at all: he was just a hopeless, scrawny junkie who couldn't play the bass-guitar that was strung low-and-cool around his waist, to save his life. And, most tragic of all for the poster-boy of the blank-generation: Sid's bass-lines on the *Sex Pistols*' 1977 album *Never Mind the Bollocks* had to be performed by guitar-thug-supreme, Steve Jones; such was Sid's overwhelming musical ineptitude. And so, I elected to get on with my life – which basically meant *still* obsessing over punk and new-wave (as I do to this day), but also getting acquainted with the other important things in life: beer and birds.

As is the case for all of us, time passed quickly, and before I knew it, the summer of 1981 rolled around and my education at the very *Grange Hill*-like Pelsall Comprehensive School – if you can call it an education – was over. My exam-results at sixteen were hardly impressive. In fact, they were practically non-existent. There were no O-Levels, A-Levels or degrees for me; just a few CSE Grade 4 and 5's, and that was it. I decided to stay on at school for an extra year to try and rectify the situation to some degree; but it was all to absolutely no avail: my like-minded mates and I simply sat around the 6th-Form room all day, drinking tea, playing cards, listening to *Radio 1*, and generally doing just about anything aside from going to lessons. It was inevitable, therefore, that I would have to walk out before I got thrown out – which is actually, and precisely, what occurred, just before the start of the six-week-long holiday midway through 1982.

For some odd reason, I can still vividly remember exactly – and I *do* mean exactly – the process of events: I packed my duffle-bag at lunchtime in the aforementioned 6th Form room, told my mates that I would see them at the nearby *George & Dragon* pub for a much-needed Saturday night piss-up (back then, landlords didn't care about I.D. cards, or if you were 18 or over), and then headed for the exit; all to the accompaniment of *Favourite Shirts* by *Haircut 100* that was playing on the radio in the background.

As I was on the verge of leaving the room, I had one last look back and saw Sharon, a Clare Grogan-lookalike (in her *Gregory's Girl* days), and the first girl I ever kissed – during a game of *Spin-the-Bottle*, at a friend's house late on a Saturday night years before – looking mournfully in my direction. I tried to smile and waved. Sharon simply ran to the coat-room, by now in full-on tears-mode. I walked out the building, knew that a significant part of my youth was over, and realized I had better get my act together while I still could.

Frankly, I had no idea what awaited me, or, even, what my plans might be. But, of one thing I was absolutely certain; namely that the words of the mighty *Sex Pistols* summed up my situation perfectly: 'Don't know what I want, but I know how to get it.' In other words, I had failed miserably at school, but, deep inside, I knew there was something out there for me. There *had* to be. But: what?

I racked my brain and thought, thought and thought again. Although I was hardly the best or most successful student, I had always loved reading: I had grown up on C.S. Lewis' tales of Narnia; Enid Blyton's *Secret Seven*; Conan Doyle's Sherlock Holmes stories; and the literary, fantasy-driven output of Alan Garner. Of course, it went without saying that I was nowhere even remotely near their heady level, but I felt that I was at least capable of stringing together a sentence or several. Was it possible, I mused, that I might also enter the realm of writing? As luck – or perhaps fate – would have it, a fortnight or thereabouts later I was sitting glumly in the local job-centre, awaiting an appointment with a no-doubt-unsmiling official of the then-much-hated and scorned Department of Health and Social Security: the DHSS.

'So, Nick: what do you want to do?' asked the definitive civil-servant sat opposite me.

'Don't know,' I said, sullenly. 'I like to read. I like to write stuff: stories.'

The woman wasn't impressed: 'Not much call for writers in Walsall, Nick.' Frankly, I wasn't in the mood for her sarcasm, and was about to say something violent and hostile in response, when, while shuffling through a pile of papers, she suddenly said words to the effect of: 'Hang on, I might have something.' And, she most certainly did have something: an eighteen-month-long, Youth Opportunities Programme (YOP) position with a local company that was launching a new community magazine in the area called *Zero*. Its aim was to provide 'the kids' with their very own publication that would cater to the things that were important to them in life: music, fashion and going out and having a good old, rip-roaring time.

'How does that sound?' the DHSS lady asked. I replied that it actually sounded pretty good, as thoughts of becoming the next Woodward & Bernstein whirled and swirled around my head. I left the DHSS on a definitive high (and I hadn't even smoked anything – yet).

Later that night – it was a Friday night, I remember very well - I met up with my best mates David Lea and David Baxter in Pelsall's *Swan* pub for a celebratory drink, or quite a few (and who, to very this day, I still meet up with down the boozer a couple of times a year, when I fly back to the U.K.).

I was very pleasantly surprised to bump into Sharon - who was out with her friends – and, afterwards, had a lengthy and welcome snog with her behind the back-doors of the pub, against a pile of empty lager-barrels. The two of us then made our way to the chippie and devoured our fish-suppers. Practically immediately afterwards, Sharon threw-up, and I half-carried her home to her Mum and Dad; who – on opening the door, after I had rung the bell – proceeded to give me an ear-splitting tirade of abuse for 'getting our daughter drunk'. Yep: enchanting Brontë/Austen-style romance was alive and kicking in Walsall; and, all in all, things were actually looking pretty good!

As it transpired, I had the job with *Zero* for nearly two years, during which time I learned much about the world of freelance writing, about the power of blagging, promotion, marketing and selling stories, about how to capture the attention of the reader and much more too. Indeed, it was as much a lesson in life as it was a tutoring in journalism. I also learned how infinitely precarious the world of writing can be.

After *Zero* imploded and folded, and as the Orwellian year of 1984 kicked-off and progressed, I struggled to find my feet and went through a veritable plethora of jobs: van-driver, shelf-stacker, forklift-driver, petrol-pump attendant, insurance-salesman and more. But, it was all to no avail: writing was by now my passion. And, slowly but surely, I returned to that world.

Since those early and formative years, I have managed to ensure that writing remains both my passion and my career. I can't say that it hasn't been a bumpy ride at times – it most certainly has; and quite regularly, too. As anyone who pursues a life in freelance-writing will attest, unless you are prepared to stay on top of things and bust a gut, it can be a harsh, bleak world. But would I change things? Not at all: thanks to my work as a writer, I have made some fabulous friends, including the editor of this very book, Jon Downes, as well as Richard Freeman, Greg Bishop, Raven Meindel, Ken Gerhard and Matthew Williams. And, of course, had I not accepted that position with *Zero*, I would likely never have met my beloved wife, Dana. Nor would we now be living on the other side of the world in sunny, pistol-packing Dallas; the home of J.R. Ewing, Sue-Ellen, Miss Ellie and the Kennedy assassination.

I've had the pleasure of writing twenty books, and numerous articles for a wealth of paranor-

Twenty-eight years after we celebrated
my job with *Zero*, the lads still hit the town!

mal publications – including *UFO Magazine*; *Fate*; *Fortean Times*; *Alien Encounters*; *Beyond*; and *Paranormal*. I have freelanced for the *Daily Express*; written features for the *Big Issue* (really!); penned columns on hot, lesbian vampires for *Penthouse*; and more. In other words, it has been a wild, fun and extraordinary time.

But, as things all began back in 1982, with *Zero*, it is to that long-gone time that we must first necessarily travel.

Two final things: first, since some background data may be useful, I have penned a small introduction to each piece, outlining how and why I came to write them.

And, second: you may well be wondering why on earth this anthology is titled *Space Girl Dead on Spaghetti Junction*. Well, I'll tell you: for a very brief, but very wonderful, period in the winter of 1981, there existed a new-wave band in Walsall called the *Poor Little Jimmy's* (who took their name from the *Undertones'* classic song *Jimmy, Jimmy*).

They were a great combination of the *Undertones* themselves, the *Freshies*, the *Members*, the *Skids*, the *Vapors*, and the *Only Ones*. And, *Leader of the Alien Pack* – a line from which the title of this book is taken - was arguably the best of their 3 or 4 self-penned, rhythm-guitar-driven tunes.

It was a classic, catchy, new-wave/lost-love ode to a beautiful space girl who meets her untimely death, late one night, when her UFO crashes on that dreadful mass of road known to one and all as Spaghetti Junction. It should have been a hit. It wasn't. It should have made the band huge. It didn't. But, lads: some of us still remember you, and were even inspired to title a book after you!

Nick Redfern
March 2011

Zero-Hour 1982/1983

The very first thing I ever did for the premier issue of the aforementioned *Zero* was to design the cover-image. It wasn't a big or difficult job at all: it just consisted of me photocopying my hand, then placing a cut-out of a map of the local area over the palm of my copied-hand and re-photocopying it. And, aside from adding some Letraset text to the cover-page, that was basically it. But, my 17-year-old mind told me I had finally arrived in the exciting world of journalism!

My second task for issue 1 was to prepare a brief editorial that went as follows:

This is *Zero*, a new community magazine which will cater specifically for young people's needs in the area. The mag will contain such articles as all the latest fashion news, local gig guides, record reviews, gig reviews and there will be a chance for readers to put forward what they would like to see in the magazine. *Zero* is produced by Robert Bakewell; Caroline Hall; Barbara Hyde; Nick Redfern; Collette Taylor; and Trevor Waddison.'

And my final job for numero-uno: to compile the gig guide, which included dates for a wide and varied range of artists that were touring at the time, including the *Anti-Nowhere League*

OPPOSITE: My first journalistic job - designing the cover of the premier issue of *Zero*..

(good); *Chelsea* (forgotten *Pistols* wannabes); *Ultravox* (so-so); *Echo and the Bunnymen* (okay); *Shakatak* (no comment at all); *Hot Gossip* (gyrating babes from Kenny Everett's show); and 'rock-chick' Pat Benatar. In other words, my first submissions equated to a distinctly mixed-bag.

Follow-up articles from me for future issues of *Zero* included a piece on local synthesiser-musician Paul Nova, who put out various recordings at the time, including *Julie Ann*, *Trees without Leaves*, and *Fantasy and Feeling*. I also recall preparing some conspiratorial commentary about the fish in a nearby canal allegedly being poisoned as a result of the beyond-carefree attitude of a local waste-disposal company.

I was on my way…sort of!

Saucer Files Exposed 1986

In 1986, I made my first visit to the Public Record Office at Kew (today, re-titled as the National Archive), and succeeded in digging out a couple of old UFO reports that had made their way to the Air Ministry; including one that, curiously enough, had been declassified some years in advance of the terms of the Government's 'Thirty Year Ruling', and which I included in a 1986 article for Mark and Graham Birdsall's, Quest, titled Saucer Files Exposed:

In mid-January 1963, the Wiltshire town of Corsham was the scene of a notable UFO encounter involving a retired Royal Air Force officer whose report attracted the attention of Air Intelligence at the MoD.

On the morning of 15 January 1963 Mr. J.E. Hipkin of Chippenham telephoned the Station Adjutant at RAF Colerne to report an unusual experience that had occurred the previous afternoon. Following established guidelines, the S.A. at Colerne asked him to submit a report in writing. It was at shortly after 5.30 p.m. on 14 January 1963.

Mr. Hipkin said when something decidedly unusual caught his eye in the sky over the town. He began:

> 'The object was a dull orange glow terminating with a tail of light of considerable length; the tail being for the best part parallel but ending in a point. As the point source of the orange glow appeared to be the rear of

the vehicle and therefore an outlet, it was perhaps significant that I could not see any shape whatever ahead of the glow. There was no audible sound whatever.'

Mr. Hipkin elaborated further:

'I estimated that I held the object in view for approximately five seconds during which it passed through an arc at a steady altitude and a phenomenal speed. My estimate of the altitude is certainly not more than three hundred feet and I place the nearest point of passing at some two thousand yards distant. The course of the object was almost due north; perhaps a few degrees east of north.

'Upon reflection one point comes to mind, as the object moved towards the point where it passed from sight I did not observe any change in intensity of light as one may possibly expect when the rear of the motor is presented to the eye. This I find odd in itself when considering the character of the subject.'

Mr. Hipkin then made a highly significant point.

'Perhaps I should say that I have served almost fifteen years in the RAF as a S.N.C.O. * and have no small experience of aircraft. Whatever the object was I feel quite sure it was not an aircraft in the accepted senses nor was it debris entering the earth's atmosphere. Living in this area I am accustomed to seeing a large amount of Air Traffic and I cannot relate this sighting to any normal flying machine.' He concluded: 'I have been careful not to colour my story with exaggeration or wishful thinking and look forward to hearing more of this matter.'

From RAF Colerne, Mr. Hipkin's report found its way to the Air Ministry at Whitehall and ultimately to Air Intelligence. The witness, it concluded, had merely been mistaken by nothing more sinister than the Echo II space satellite. Of course, it is quite true that people do mistake satellites in earth orbit for something potentially far more exotic; however, it should not be forgotten that in this case, the witness was a trained observer with the Royal Air Force of fifteen years standing. Not only that, he was adamant that the object was at a height of no more than three thousand feet and at one point came within two thousand yards of his location. It goes without saying that if a satellite were to come within two thousand yards of British soil, a calamity of unprecedented proportions would occur microseconds later when it would inevitably slam into the ground!

Whatever the truth of the matter, Mr. Hipkin was informed of the Air Ministry's conclusion and the report was quietly filed away in the Ministry's archives.

---

* Author's Note: Senior Non-Commissioned Officer

Fatherly Words 1987

As I noted above, it was 1986 when I began writing for the old *Quest* journal put out by Graham and Mark Birdsall (that eventually became *UFO Magazine*). And, after having written 5 or 6 articles for *Quest* (all now, unfortunately, lost to the fog of time and the dustbin – unless you happen to possess your own copies of those long-gone items), I prepared the following, which, in various, updated and expanded incarnations, served as the prologue to my 1997 book, *A Covert Agenda*, and as stand-alone articles in various glossy magazines of the 1990s and 2000s. But, the following is the 1987 original:

As someone who writes about UFOs and other weird things, I am sometimes asked: How did you become interested and involved in the worlds of the unexplained and the paranormal? It was 10.30 p.m. on a dark Wednesday evening in late 1978 as I walked with my father, Frank Redfern, through the deserted streets of the town of Walsall. A biting wind sliced through the air and I buried my hands in my coat pockets in a vain attempt to keep warm. We headed for a nearby car park.

'Well, what did you think?' asked my father.

'I thought it was great,' I replied, continuing: 'do you think it could really happen?'

My father looked at me out of the corner of his eye; and a knowing smile crossed his face: 'Maybe it already has,' he replied, his voice dropping ever so slightly.

The subject of this cryptic conversation: Steven Spielberg's classic film, *Close Encounters Of The Third Kind*, which told the story of humankind's first face-to-face meeting with an alien species, and that we had just seen at Walsall's *ABC* cinema. We climbed the stairs of the car park and headed for my father's *Ford Capri* car, and my thirteen-year-old mind mused upon his comment.

'What did you mean by that?' I asked in reference to his curious words.

'Hang on,' he replied. 'Let's get out of the car park and I'll tell you,' he said. And as we drove home on that late autumn evening, the startling facts surrounding my father's involvement in the UFO subject came tumbling out.

Like the majority of young men in Britain in the 1950s, my father was required to serve a three-year-term in the military under British National Service regulations. Because of his keen interest in aviation, he chose the Royal Air Force. During his service with the RAF, he served at various RAF stations, but by far the most memorable experience of his career occurred near the East Coast of England at a place called RAF Neatishead, Norfolk.

It was September 1952 and my father was working as a radar mechanic.

'So what happened?' I asked, as we drove home.

'Well,' he began, 'I remember that we were taking part in an exercise – Mainbrace, it was called – and I was on duty. It was early in the morning – four or five o'clock – maybe a bit later. Things were pretty normal until the radar picked up something on the scopes.'

'What was it?' I asked eagerly.

'At first,' he explained, 'we thought it might have been an aircraft, but we knew soon enough that it was something else. We had this object, this UFO, whatever you want to call it, on the scopes at fifty thousand feet, and flying over the North Sea and parallel to the English coast. The speed of it meant there was no way this was a plane.'

He continued: 'The report went up the chain, and aircraft were scrambled from Coltishall – which was a base nearby. Coltishall sent up Venom and Meteor aircraft to try and get a look at the object. We were watching all this on the screens thinking that it would turn out to be some-

My dad, Frank Redfern, who introduced me to the world of the UFO.

thing ordinary. But when the planes closed in, the UFO suddenly streaked away and headed towards Norway. The pilots didn't have a chance.

'The next day,' he added, 'something strange happened. A bunch of people came – a photographic team from Coltishall – and they had some really good gear which they set up to record the radar's Plan Position Indicator tube in case the UFO came back. Well, the day following this, it did come back. We tracked it; the planes went up, but this time we had it all on film.'

'What happened then?' I wondered.

My father replied: 'We never knew. The guys from Coltishall removed everything: the radar tapes, the records, all of it. Everyone was told not to discuss it outside of the base. They never told us what the result was, and the UFO never came back, but I won't forget it.'

I sat back in the car-seat, amazed at what I had just heard. UFOs – so often the subject of ridicule – really existed. And, more significantly, Britain's military knew it too. The remainder of the journey was made in silence; me trying to take in these remarkable facts and my father recalling his long-gone days with the Royal Air Force.

Today, my father still vividly recalls the events of September 1952 and is convinced that something truly strange did indeed occur to both him and his colleagues on those fateful nights. I agree. And, were it not for my father, I would not have set out on the journey that has ultimately led me here. Thanks, Dad.

The Beckenham Ball of Light 1990

Thus was titled an article I prepared for a couple of Midlands-based Fortean newsletters in 1990, and which later got picked up by several more self-published magazines, if memory serves me right – and I believe it does. It's not a long article, but the case is a thought-provoking one:

Midway through 1963, an event occurred at Beckenham, Kent, that bore all the hallmarks of an encounter with one of the fabled Foo Fighters of the Second World War. And the witness had a military background: he had served during the hostilities of 1939-45 with an anti-aircraft detachment and until 1961, was attached to a territorial unit of the British Army.

As Mr. W. Hooper informed the Air Ministry:

> 'At 0150 hrs on Tuesday the 27th August I was awakened by my wife to see what appeared to be something in flames falling from the sky, slightly N.W. of my house. This object appeared to be a ball of incandescent gas, red and black and was about a foot in diameter, and gave the impression of intense heat. It dropped like a stone from approximately 1000 ft to 500 ft, then stayed still for about 2-3 seconds, then started moving at an incredible speed in a Northerly direction and was out of sight in a matter of about 4 seconds. As it went away the wind brought a slight humming sound to us and the red and black appearance turned slightly yellow.
>
> 'I would be grateful if you could throw any light on the matter for me and would like especially to know if you had anything showing on your radar screens at the time I have stated. I am convinced that the object was pow-

> ered as it travelled against the wind, and think what we saw may have been some sort of exhaust gas or flame.'

Possibly anticipating that Whitehall would offer a totally down-to-earth explanation for what occurred, Mr. Hooper closed his letter thus: 'I hope you will not try and persuade me that the object was a meteorological balloon as these as far as I know could not possibly travel against the wind.'

In this particular case, Air Intelligence once again asserted that a solution had been found. Mr. Hooper, came back the conclusion, had been fooled by a 'fireball'. That the UFO had hovered in the air for two to three seconds was ignored by Air Intelligence; as was the fact that Mr. Hooper's anti-aircraft work during the Second World War would have given him first-class observational skills.

MJ12: The FBI Connection 1993

In the final month of 1993, I submitted an article – titled *MJ12: The FBI Connection* – to numerous publications. It was an article that told the odd saga of how and why the FBI came to investigate the notorious MJ12 documents that kept many a ufologist busy for years. This was, of course, pre-Internet days; and so my article found its way across Britain and the United States via mail and fax. I know that, in the months that followed, it appeared in 3 or 4 magazines and newsletters – and maybe there were others, too. Anyway, here's the piece in its entirety:

Howard Blum is an award-winning author and former New York Times journalist, twice nominated by the editors of that newspaper for the Pulitzer Prize in Investigative Reporting. In 1990, Blum's book *Out There* was published and detailed his investigation of U.S. military and governmental involvement in the UFO subject. According to Blum, on 4 June 1987, the UFO skeptic Philip J. Klass wrote to William Baker, Assistant Director at the Office of Congressional and Public Affairs. "I am enclosing what purport to be Top Secret/Eyes Only documents, which have not been properly declassified, now being circulated by William L. Moore, Burbank, California, 91505…" The Bureau swung into action.

Jacques Vallee - the UFO author, investigator, and former principal investigator on Department of Defense computer networking projects - stated in his book *Revelations* that the FBI turned away from the MJ12 documents in "disgust" and professed no interest in the matter. Papers and comments made to me by the FBI and the Air Force Office of Special Investigations, however, reflect a totally different scenario. Furthermore, there are indications that the

FBI launched (or were at least involved in) several MJ12-linked investigations during the late 1980s.

Of those investigations, one definitely began in the latter part of 1988. Howard Blum has stated that of those approached by the FBI "in the fall of 1988," one was a "Working Group" established under the auspices of the Defense Intelligence Agency tasked with looking at the UFO subject. In 1990, Blum was interviewed by *UFO Magazine* and was asked if the Working Group could have been a "front" for another even more covert investigative body within the government. Blum's response aptly sums up one of the major problems faced by both those inside and outside of government when trying to determine exactly who knows what.

"Interestingly," said Blum, "members of [the Working Group] aired that possibility themselves. When looking into the MJ12 papers, some members of the group said - and not in jest – 'Perhaps we're just a front organization for some sort of MJ12. Suppose, in effect, we conclude the MJ12 papers are phony, are counterfeit. Then we've solved the entire mystery for the government, relieving them of the burden in dealing with it, and at the same time, we allow the real secret to remain held by a higher source.' An FBI agent told me there are so many secret levels within the government that even the government isn't aware of it!"

A separate Autumn investigation in 1988 was conducted by the FBI's Foreign Counter-Intelligence division and operated out of Washington and New York. Some input into the investigation also came from the FBI office in Dallas, Texas; the involvement of the latter confirmed to me by Oliver B. Revell, Special Agent in Charge at Dallas FBI.

On 15 September 1988, an agent of the Air Force Office of Special Investigations contacted Dallas FBI and supplied the Bureau with another copy of the MJ12 papers. This set was obtained from a source whose identity, according to documentation released to me by the Bureau, the Airforce Office of Special Investigations (AFOSI) has deemed must remain classified to this day.

Before addressing the involvement of the FBI's Foreign Counter-Intelligence division in this matter, let us focus our attention on Dallas FBI. On 25 October 1988, the Dallas office transmitted a two-page Secret Airtel to headquarters that read as follows:

> "Enclosed for the Bureau is an envelope which contains a possible classified document. Dallas notes that within the last six weeks, there has been local publicity regarding 'OPERATION MAJESTIC-12' with at least two appearances on a local radio talk show, discussing the MAJESTIC-12 OPERATION, the individuals involved, and the Government's attempt to keep it all secret. It is unknown if this is all part of a publicity campaign. [Censored] from OSI, advises that `OPERATION BLUE BOOK`, mentioned in the document on page 4 did exist. Dallas realizes that the purported document is over 35 years old, but does not know if it has been properly declassified. The Bureau is requested to discern if the document is still classified. Dallas will hold any investigation in abeyance until further direction from FBIHQ."

Partly as a result of the actions of the Dallas FBI Office and partly as a result of the investigation undertaken by the FBI's Foreign Counter-Intelligence people, on 30 November 1988 an arranged meeting took place in Washington D.C. between agents of the Bureau and those of AFOSI. If the AFOSI had information on MJ12, said the Bureau, they would like to know.

A Secret communication back to the Dallas office from Washington on 2 December 1988 read:

> "This communication is classified Secret in its entirety. Reference Dallas Airtel dated October 25 1988. Reference Airtel requested that FBIHQ determine if the document enclosed by referenced Airtel was classified or not. The Office of Special Investigations, US Air Force, advised on November 30, 1988, that the document was fabricated. Copies of that document have been distributed to various parts of the United States. The document is completely bogus. Dallas is to close captioned investigation."

At first glance, that would seem to lay matters to rest once and for all. Unfortunately, it does not. There can be no dispute that the Air Force has played a most strange game with respect to MJ12. The FBI was assured by AFOSI that the MJ12 papers were "fabricated, a hoax" and were not leaked, official documents. However, Special Agent Frank Batten, Jr., chief of the Information Release Division at the Investigative Operations Center with the USAF, admitted to me on 30 April 1993 that AFOSI is not now maintaining (nor ever has maintained) any records pertaining to either MJ12, or any investigation thereof. This begs an important question. How was AFOSI able to determine that the papers were faked if no investigation on their part was undertaken? Batten has also advised me that while AFOSI *did* "discuss" the MJ12 documents with the FBI, incredibly they made absolutely no written reference to that meeting in any shape or form. This is most odd: government and military agencies are methodical when it comes to documenting possible breaches of security.

Richard L. Weaver, formerly the Deputy for Security and Investigative Programs with the U.S. Air Force (and the author of the US Air Force's 1995 near-1000 page report, *The Roswell Report: Fact Vs. Fiction in the New Mexico Desert*), advised me similarly on 12 October 1993. "The Air Force considers the MJ12 (both the group described and the purported documents) to be bogus," stated Weaver. He, too, conceded, however, that there were "no documents responsive" to my request for Air Force files on how just such a determination was reached. Stanton Friedman has also stated that, based on his correspondence with Weaver on the issue of MJ12, he too is dissatisfied with the responses that he received after filing similar FOIA requests relating to the way in which the Air Force made its "bogus" determination.

Moreover, there is the fact that AFOSI informed the FBI that, "copies of that document have been distributed to various parts of the United States." To make such a statement AFOSI simply must have conducted some form of investigation or have been in receipt of data from yet another agency with knowledge of the affair.

If the Bureau learned anything further about MJ12 in the post-1989 period, then that information has not surfaced under the terms of the Freedom of Information Act. Perhaps the Bureau, unable to get satisfactory answers from the military and the intelligence community, simply gave up the chase. Thanks to Richard L. Huff, Bureau Co-Director within the Office of Information and Privacy, it can be determined that MJ12 remains the subject of an FBI headquarters Main File that is titled "Espionage." Today that file is in "closed status."

The enigma of MJ12, meanwhile, continues.

Unexplained Ground Marking and UFO Incident 1995

Well, if you're wondering what that strange mouthful is all about, I'll tell you: it was the title of an article from me on an intriguing crop circle-type event that occurred in early 1964 in the north of England – an event that even caught the attention of the Ministry of Defence! I had found the official documentation on the case at the National Archive, while digging through a three-hundred-page-plus file on UFO sightings reported to the MoD throughout 1964. I prepared an article on the curious affair that appeared in a number of publications, including (first) a very short-lived, West Midlands-based newsletter titled *Tales from the Hangar* (in mid-1995) then in Jenny Randles' *Northern UFO News* (in November of that same year), and, later, in the Winter 1996 issue of *The Crop Watcher*. And, this is it:

In accordance with the British Government's 'Thirty Year Ruling', a three-hundred-page file of UFO reports, covering the period 1963-4, has recently been declassified and made available for inspection at the Public Record Office, Kew. Although the overwhelming majority of the file (which originated with a now-defunct Air Ministry secretariat, S4) is devoted to routine matters, such as responding to enquiries from UFO researchers, and examining 'lights in the sky'-type reports submitted to the Air Ministry by members of the public, there are several incidents which stand out as being potentially important. One such incident occurred during mid-March 1964 and may well have a bearing on the crop circle mystery.

On 23 March 1964, T.E.T. Burbury, the Rector at Clifton Rectory, Penrith, Cumberland, wrote to the National Physical Laboratory at Teddington describing an encounter which had occurred some days previously. I quote from the Rector's letter:

> 'Dear Sirs: Does an apparent column of blue light about 8' in diameter and about 15' feet high which disappears and leaves a mark of very slightly disturbed earth, the same diameter, mean anything to you? This occurred about 9.30 p.m. last Saturday night about 2 miles from here. It was seen by a person who is very short sighted who would have been unable to see anything, except the light, even if it had been present.
>
> 'I examined the ground which is about 100 Yds from the nearest building and there are no pylons near. There was no sign of burning, either by sight or smell, the grass growing between the exposed ground appeared quite normal. There were no signs of bird tracks or droppings: the ground simply appeared to have been lightly raked over in an almost perfect circle.
>
> 'For your information only, I told the farmer to have a sample of the earth collected and analysed for bacteria content, but don't know whether he has done so. Yours faithfully: T.E.T. Burbury.'

'…the ground simply appeared to have been lightly raked over in an almost perfect circle', said the Rector. Does this not sound somewhat familiar? Furthermore, Burbury's reference to 'the farmer' strongly suggests that the circle was found on farmland. And: what of the column of blue light?

Realising that this was out of their jurisdiction, staff at the National Physical Laboratory forwarded a copy of the rector's letter to the Meteorological Office at London Road, Bracknell. In turn, H.M. Race of the Meteorological Office advised Burbury that: 'This does not appear to be a meteorological matter and we are therefore passing your letter to a London office who may be able to deal with it.'

The 'London office' to which Race was referring was the aforementioned S4. For its part, S4 seemed largely unconcerned, even amused by the rector's report, as the following memorandum of 16 April 1964 from R.A, Langton of S4 to a colleague, Flight Lieutenant A. Bardsley shows: 'I should be grateful for your advice on the report in the attached correspondence. Could it be Will o' the Wisp?'

Two months later, Flight Lieutenant Bardsley stated the following in a good-humoured 'Loose Minute' to Mr. Langton:

> 'This is quite a corker! The explanation could be one of several things, depending really, on the state of the investigator's liver. One explanation

OPPOSITE: Before Crop Circles there were...Crop Circles!

The Mowing-Devil:

Or, Strange NEWS out of

Hartford-shire.

Being a True Relation of a Farmer, who Bargaining with a Poor Mower, about the Cutting down Three Half-Acres of Oats: upon the Mower's asking too much, the Farmer swore, That the Devil should Mow it, rather than He. And so it fell out, that that very Night, the Crop of Oats shew'd as if it had been all of a Flame: but next Morning appear'd so neatly Mow'd by the Devil, or some Infernal Spirit, that no Mortal Man was able to do the like. Also, How the said Oats ly now in the Field, and the Owner has not Power to fetch them away.

Licensed, August 22th, 1678.

could be aurora borealis. This phenomenon, however, is so unpredictable that it would be rather hopeless to expect someone to have seen the aurora at the same date/time as our short-sighted observer. Professor Paton at Edinburgh is an aurora expert, but I cannot really justify pestering him with this one. Again your "will o' the wisp" theory may be correct. However whilst following this line, the Royal Geographic Society confirmed that Penrith did not exist – at least in Bradshaw's Gazetteer. Further, information on the geological structure around Penrith again confirmed that there probably would not, but possibly could be, local ignitions of methane gas – absolutely no use these experts! Our myopic observer may possibly have seen car headlights shining up into a low cloud base. There is no mention of any sound in this report – could the observer be also deaf! One comment by the rector intrigues me: Could it be the rector thinks the object could be a phoenix? Finally: There once was a rector of Penrith, who reported that one of his Kith, saw blue light in the night, got a terrible fright, and the rector thinks it's a "myth."'

Although Flight Lieutenant Bardsley signed off his 'Loose Minute' in fine poetic style, he did not see fit to comment on the 'almost perfect circle' reported by the rector, nor did he express an interest in following up on the rector's suggestion to the farmer that a sample of earth should be collected for study. Moreover, an examination of the Air Ministry file in question reveals no further reference to this particular case, and to the best of my knowledge, the entire matter appears to have been summarily dismissed. To my way of thinking, this seems somewhat curious.

Of course, it should not be forgotten that the only papers to which we currently have access originated with S4. Flight Lieutenant Bardsley, however, was attached to the Defence Intelligence Staff – a wholly separate division whose work is highly compartmented. Indeed, I was informed by the Public Record Office in 1994 that the overwhelming majority of all papers which originated with the DIS remain exempt from disclosure. 'These records,' I was told, 'are retained because they contain information relating to the security and intelligence agencies and are obviously highly sensitive.'

In light of this, perhaps we should not dismiss the possibility that the DIS built up its own file on the case; a file which has still to see the light of day. While this is simply speculation on my part, it is speculation which should not be discarded out of hand.

More importantly, now that we know the approximate location of the 'circle' (around two miles from Clifton Rectory), perhaps some enterprising researcher will do the necessary follow-up work and track down the Reverend Burbury and the unnamed farmer – presuming, of course, that they are still alive. If they are, their recollections may prove vital in furthering our understanding of the 'crop circle' mystery.

UFOs over Staffordshire 1996

Back in 1996, I toyed with the idea of writing a book on the somewhat enigmatic 'Flying Triangle' aspect of Ufology; but, I got so tied up with my books *A Covert Agenda* (published in 1997) and *The FBI Files* (which surfaced in the following year) that I never actually got around to doing anything about it. But, had I done so, I would most certainly have included the following – which I prepared for the 'Triangle Book' back in late '96. The case at issue is that of a good friend of mine named Tracie Austin-Peters, formerly of Stoke-on-Trent and now a resident of Sin-City itself: Las Vegas, Nevada. As many within British Ufology may recall, Tracie (who Andy Roberts once described in the most excellent and utterly scandalous *Armchair Ufologist* as a dead-ringer for Celine Dion) was seemingly ever-present at UFO gigs up and down the land, and would often travel with me and Irene Bott, of the *Staffordshire UFO Group*, to events and places far and wide. And with that said, here's the strange tale of Tracie's very own 1996 encounter of a distinctly Flying Triangle variety:

O f the many UFO reports that caught my attention in 1996, one of the most fascinating came from Tracie Austin-Peters, a (then) North Staffordshire-based businesswoman. 'It was about 3 o'clock in the afternoon on May 14, 1996,' states Tracie today,

> 'and it was quite a clear and sunny day. I'd got about an hour and a half free before I had to be back at work and decided that, because it was so nice, I would drive up to a wood nearby with a book and read for a while.
>
> 'Well, I headed for the local shop and pulled up on the car park, as I was going to get a few items to take with me. But as I got out of the car I got an immediate urge to look up. It was just like something had told me to look

up – although I didn't hear a voice. It was more like an impulse. And I knew directly where to look, too. And as I looked up, I saw a really unusual shaped object that was shaped like a boomerang or a v-shape. It was silent, it was black; and as I stood watching it, I thought to myself: I need to get a grip on this! What am I looking at?'

Tracie continues:

'I'm quite a logical person, and I wondered at first if it was a large bird of some kind, but it wasn't. The wings were just stretched out and it wasn't moving like a bird. It was sort of turning anti-clockwise. And it certainly wasn't an aeroplane or a hang-glider. I knew I had to grab someone to see if they could see it, too.

'There was a woman near me getting her child out of her car and I said to her: "Excuse me, I hope you don't think I'm being silly, but can you see what I can see in the sky?" She replied: "You mean that black thing?" I said, "Yes!" and we both stood and watched it. But I got a very strong feeling, like it was giving off a thought, saying: "Have a good look at me because what you are seeing is real."'

At that point, something truly strange occurred:

'I watched it and then it did the most bizarre thing. It shrunk itself into a black sphere but continued to move anti-clockwise. But the strange thing was that the lady who was with me didn't see it change shape.

'I thought this was ridiculous and ran across the car park to grab someone else. He saw it, too, but didn't know what it was. But as I watched, the object then transformed from a square back to its original shape and then an appendage came out of the middle, which made it look like an arrowhead.

'It then headed off in what I thought was the direction of the woods. So, I jumped in the car, headed off there, too. I scanned the sky but didn't see it again unfortunately. Well, I was due to start work again about 4.30 p.m., so I went home and telephoned Irene Bott of the *Staffordshire UFO Group* and told her what had happened. Irene told me to write it all down and draw a picture of the object – which I did. I also phoned a local UFO group in my area, too, and they said they would look into it.

'Suddenly, at that point, I got this feeling again to look up in the sky and was amazed to see this same object flying directly over my house! It was so strange; I wasn't frightened – just surprised and excited. And the whole thing took on such a magical atmosphere. And again, I got the feeling that the object wanted to be seen. I'm not too brilliant at heights, but it was much lower than your average aircraft. Again, it was moving in an anti-clockwise way and I watched it until it vanished.'

Hanging out with Tracie Austin-Peters.

The story was not quite over, however.

> 'Three days later, the UFO group phoned me back to say that they had had a call from a guy who didn't want to leave his name but who lived about four miles from me. They told me that he said he'd seen three black boomerang-shaped objects flying over his house, and I just couldn't believe it.'

To this day, Tracie says, the extraordinary events of 14 May 1996 remain firmly fixed in her mind and she is adamant that something truly out-of-this-world took place.

The Rising of the Moon 1997

Over the years, I've written quite a few introductions and forewords for the books of friends and colleagues (such as for Linda Godfrey's *Hunting the American Werewolf*; the late Mac Tonnies' *The Cryptoterrestrials*; *Hidden Headlines of Texas* by Chad Lewis; and – even! – *Mind Controlled Sex Slaves*, published by Tim Green Beckley, and which also contains data from the notorious *Commander X*!); however, the very first foreword I wrote was for *The Rising of the Moon*; the 1997 title of Jon Downes and Nigel Wright that is truly Fortean in nature and scope. If you haven't read the book (and, if you haven't, then you really should!), you can get an idea of it from my original foreword below:

As someone who is a firm believer in the theory that some UFOs are extraterrestrial spacecraft, I have given much thought as to why I elected to write the foreword for *The Rising of the Moon* – a book that postulates so manifestly different a theory to explain the ever-present UFO mystery on our planet.

Primarily, there are three reasons: first, Jon is a good mate, and unlike so many other people I've come across in the UFO and paranormal fields, he has a fine sense of humour; second, there was the lure of a copious amount of free alcohol and a selection of *Ramones* bootlegs from Jon's vast and varied record collection; and third (and certainly most important of all), his book is a damn fine read – at times funny, disturbing, tragic and, ultimately, cathartic.

But what can I say about the book without giving too much away to the unsuspecting reader? Well…if you thought that you had spent your hard-earned wages/giro (delete as applicable) on a straightforward 'UFO book' you would be very wrong. *Rising of the Moon* is anything *but* a straightforward UFO book! Rather, it is an intensely personal account of Jon's (and, it should not be forgotten, Nigel's) attempt to get his head round – and make some sense of – that which, in scientific terms, has come to be known collectively as 'weird shit': UFOs, animal mutilations, lake monsters, crop circles, Bigfoot, mystery big cats and all manner of associated strangeness that plagues those of us engaged in the investigation of the incredible.

Of equal significance, however, is the fact that the writing of the book also played a considerable role in Jon's ultimately successful attempts to exorcise his own personal demons – demons that took him to the very edge of sanity and very nearly to the point of no return. Moreover, Jon is to be applauded for having the balls to reveal to one and all the stark facts surrounding this aspect of his life and writing career.

So, what does Jon's quest tell us? First and foremost, as anyone who knows Jon will be aware, he not only has a love of all things Fortean, but a vast knowledge of such matters, too, and this shines throughout the text. What also shines through is Jon's dogged determination to check, recheck and cross-reference the evidence – something that is sadly lacking in much of today's paranormal research.

Jon and Nigel begin by acquainting us with the facts surrounding a spectacular wave of UFO encounters that occurred almost on his very doorstep during 1997, and goes on in workmanlike fashion to chronicle the quite-literally astounding number of reports that subsequently followed – reports encompassing strange lights zipping around the Devon and Cornwall countryside; UFOs rising out of the sea at Otter Cove; 'whale mutilations'; ghostly 'black dogs'; and strange creatures seen roaming around the wilds of the West Country.

This, as you can imagine, was no standard 'UFO wave'. Rather, it turned out to be just one piece of a very large and infinitely complex jigsaw – a jigsaw that was to stretch Jon's and Nigel's investigative skills to their limit and that, finally, led them to propose an ingenious and highly plausible theory to explain that aforementioned collection of 'weird shit'.

As someone who writes primarily about government cover-ups surrounding the UFO issue, I was also intrigued to see that Jon had also looked into a variety of rumours relating to British Government involvement in a number of purported UFO cases that Nigel had found dating back not just to the 1940s and 1950s, but also to the turn of the century when specific parts of the country were plagued by the so-called 'phantom airship mystery'. Again, Jon's ability to sort the wheat from the chaff comes to the fore, and it is refreshing to find someone who is able to address such issues without allowing their personal prejudices to come into play.

The Rising of the Moon also takes us to the furthest depths of the human psyche and gives us a disturbing look at the 'mind monsters' that very possibly lurk within all of us – and, indeed, what can happen when they break free of their constraints and begin to...well, that's something for you to discover as you read the book.

Do I agree with all Jon's conclusions? No; of course not. But that is how it should be: in a field such as this, it is vital that we (a) consider all manner of theories and beliefs; and (b) do not rule out that we might contemplate being too 'out there'. Yes, I am an adherent of the theory that we do have (or, at least, have had) extraterrestrials among us. I am also an adherent of

The Lord of the Manor himself, JD.

the belief that the U.S. Government has in its possession the remains of one or more retrieved alien spacecraft, as well as a variety of alien bodies held in suitable 'cold storage'.

As Jon and Nigel rightly note in their book, however, there are accounts dating back centuries of strange bodies (many of the 'mermaid' variety) rumoured to have been found in remote areas, only to disappear later amid claims of cover-up and confabulation. The parallels between these accounts and that relating to the so-called Roswell Incident are plain to see. Those of us who do believe that in some government facility there exists prime evidence of UFO reality, would do well to recognise that such accounts are not solely the domain of late-1940s USA.

However, the 'E.T. angle' is only one aspect of an infinitely broader mystery; and I feel confident in saying that when the full picture finally emerges into the public domain, *The Rising of the Moon* will be judged as a prophetic and highly-relevant piece of work.

So, if you enjoy reading about unidentified flying objects, fantastic beasts, strange life-forms soaring amid the upper atmosphere, dark-robed figures creeping around in the dead of night, black masses in ancient woods and much more (including what is surely the epitome of all that is unholy – Toby the dog), then Jon's book will certainly not disappoint. Indeed, it has something for everybody: the UFO devotee, the Charles Fort fanatic, the H.P. Lovecraft disciple, the Crowley crowd and just about anyone else who has ever contemplated the mysteries of our planet.

In view of its contents, however, I suggest that you read *The Rising of the Moon* by candlelight on a dark and stormy winter's night – preferably in a suitably-spooky old house on the edge of some desolate and windswept moorland. Sit yourself down with a plentiful supply of mature scrumpy and indulge in the black, disturbing and eye-opening ideas of a true visionary.

I thought about concluding my foreword in *X-Files* fashion by stating something like: 'The truth is in here', or: 'Trust no one – except Jon Downes and Nigel Wright.' Instead, I'll simply say: 'Read and enjoy; you will not be disappointed!'

A Close Encounter of the Literary Kind
1997

While digging through a file of then-recently-declassified Ministry of Defence files on UFOs at the National Archive midway through 1996, I came across an eye-opening report concerning the then-thirty-year-old sighting of a famous British author – and one that practically screamed 'BLACK HELICOPTER!!!' Yes, really. Well, when I told the Birdsall boys about my discovery, practically all hell broke loose. 'We need an article on that, lad, and quick!' came the wild screaming down the phone. So, to ensure there was no dark trouble at mill, I churned out the following, which duly hit the newsstands some time in that heady and halcyon UFO-saturated year of 1997:

According to a batch of files that the Public Record Office declassified, on 7 January 1966, the well-known writer Dame Rebecca West, MBE, was inadvertently plunged into a distinctly strange puzzle. Incredibly, she asserted, some sort of unusual aerial object, had landed in the grounds of her home – Ibstone House.

For its part, the files reveal, the Ministry of Defence was intent on playing down the case and suggested that West had simply misidentified a helicopter seen under poor conditions. Whatever the truth of the matter, West's odd experience became the subject of a fifteen-page file that attracted the attention of the elite of the MoD's Defence Intelligence Staff.

Born in 1892, Rebecca West (the adopted name of Cecily Isabel Fairfield) was the daughter of Charles Fairfield, who was renowned in London society for his spirited and witty defence of

Archives of the Unknown.

'extreme individualism' in debates with the likes of George Bernard Shaw. Whilst West was still a child, Fairfield re-located his family to Edinburgh - where he died; leaving his widow and four daughters in circumstances bordering on poverty.

West (who adopted the name Rebecca at the age of nineteen after Ibsen's heroine in *Rosmersholm*) remained in Edinburgh and continued her education there, trained briefly for the stage in London, before becoming a noted feminist and journalist – and taking much of her inspiration from the Pankhursts. As her career blossomed, West wrote for *The Freewoman*, *The Clarion* and *The New Freewoman*; and many of her pugnacious writings from that time were collated and re-printed as *The Young Rebecca* in 1932.

Her first novel, *The Return of the Soldier*, was published in 1918 and was followed by *The Judge*, *The Strange Necessity*, *Harriet June*, *The Thinking Reed*; and after an extended period, *The Fountain Overflows* and *The Birds Fall Down*. In the meantime, in 1930 West married one Henry Maxwell Andrews, a banker, who was to accompany her on the journey that ultimately led to the publication of her two-volume study of the Yugoslav nation, *The Black Lamb* and *Grey Falcon*.

West was also present at the Nuremburg trials and her 1949 book, *The Meaning of Treason*, largely grew out of articles commissioned by the *New Yorker*. In 1965, only one year before her curious UFO encounter occurred, *The Meaning of Treason* was updated with added accounts of what were then more recent scandals (including those of John Vassall, a spy in the Admiralty sentenced to eighteen years imprisonment, and Stephen Ward, a player in the Profumo case). But how did Dame Rebecca West become embroiled in the UFO controversy? As the now-aged and fading documentation at the Public Record Office reveals, it was 2.45 p.m. on 7 January 1966 and West was out walking in the grounds of her home when…

'As I was going down the steep hill to the farm buildings I noticed a man walking on my property at some distance to the right of the path I was following,' she wrote to the MoD.

> 'Presently, he reached a point when the wood stopped and there is a hedge which runs down to the valley along a sharp ridge. There is a gap in the hedge and the man stopped just past this and turned around, facing in the reverse direction, and stood still.'

Expressing concern about 'what he was going to do', West watched in amazement as what she described as 'an aerial construction' appeared out of nowhere. 'One moment it was not there, the next it was,' Rebecca West explained. 'It seemed to come down quite rapidly, on the other side of the hedge from the man, but very close to it.' And what, precisely, was it that Dame Rebecca West saw? Her description was curious, to say the least.

Stressing to the MoD that the object was 'strangely shaped', she stated:

> 'It consisted of something like a metal band, grey-blue in colour, flattened at one point so as to seem almost leaf-like, crossed with a sort of herringbone system of metal strips.'

She elaborated further:

> 'There was also somehow attached to these an odd object like a bag with an opening that had points, made of yellowish material. As I looked the whole thing collapsed toward the ground.
>
> 'I saw it crumpling downwards, but crumpling is not quite the word. The metal band seemed to cut backwards and disappear while the curious bag looked as if someone were squeezing the air out of the lower portion of it, so that all the points stood up, and then fell back. Comparing the height of the object with the height of the man, I should put it as something [between] fifteen and twenty.'

Also playing on West's mind was the identity of the mystery man. Stressing that his behaviour was 'very odd', she continued that

> 'he seemed to be watching the thing come down, and the minute it was

down, he turned round and followed the hedge track down to the valley. Once or twice he looked to his left as if he were scrutinising the valley, and he did not seem to see me. But at the bottom of the track he stopped again and looked all round the slope on which I was standing, and this time he seemed to see me. We stood and looked at each other for quite a long time, and I had an uncomfortable feeling and went home.'

The key question centred on the identity of the strange object. In her letter to the Ministry of Defence, West wrote that a farm labourer had informed her that he had seen a helicopter flying in the vicinity earlier on that same day. West, meanwhile, ventured the possibility that it was 'some gadget sent out by the Meteorological Office'.

Rebecca West signed off:

> 'I feel most apologetic for burdening you with such an improbable story. But I did not like to report it to the local police, as I think you will agree that an elderly woman who went to the local police with a story of having seen the equivalent of a flying saucer would be adding considerably to the difficulties of her life.'

On arrival at the MoD, West's letter (and accompanying drawing) was forwarded to a particular office known to have been involved in the collation of UFO data in the 1960s and referred to as s4f (Air). As the records show, however, one L.W. Akhurst of that office then dispatched all of the relevant data to a Flight Lieutenant Mercer of the Defence Intelligence Staff.

For his part, Mercer was inclined to accept that, 'Dame Rebecca West saw a helicopter, possibly of the Bell 47 or similar type, which in conditions of poor visibility appeared to have some unusual characteristics'. Despite this assertion, it is interesting to note that Mercer duly stamped his evaluation *Restricted* and advised Akhurst to inform Rebecca West of his conclusions.

Needless to say, she was far from convinced by the MoD's explanation and fired a letter back to Ackhurst.

> 'To have appeared where I saw it a helicopter would have had to fly twenty or thirty yards with its lower half deeply embedded in the earth.'

She also maintained that: 'There was at this time complete silence' and 'that visibility seemed to me not poor at all, for I spotted several birds at a considerable distance. I do not expect an answer to this letter'.

She concluded:

> 'I reported the incident partly because I feared the object might be a parachute or some such construction which was being used to drop something or somebody for criminal purposes, and partly because the construction I saw or thought I saw puzzled me, as I could not conceive how it could be got into the air, could stay in the air, or be brought down out of the air.'

Akhurst's response was short and to the point. 'No further evidence has become available concerning this particular sighting, so there is nothing further I can add.' The case was closed. For its part, the Ministry of Defence seemed satisfied with the explanation that the object was simply a helicopter. However, West's letters clearly demonstrate that not only had she summarily dismissed the notion that the object was a helicopter ('I have seen many in my time, and I can't imagine how I could have seen a helicopter from any angle which would have made it present such an appearance,' she stated), she had also given much consideration to the idea that the object was some form of man-made gadget. Yet, she was equally well aware of the fact that her report seemed to fall squarely into the Flying Saucer category too. And there was also the glaring observation on her part that the object had been flying in total silence.

Dame Rebecca West continued to write with vigour almost until the time of her death at the age of ninety in 1983, and her contribution to British literature is more than well recognised. It seems that more than thirty years on, however, this particularly curious aspect of her notable life will remain forever unresolved.

The Secret Life of Errol Flynn 1998

Today, Mark Birdsall is the editor of the espionage-based newsstand magazine, *Eye-Spy*, which he produces from his home in darkest Yorkshire. But, long before *Eye-Spy* reared its head, and got MI5 all hot and bothered (oh yes, it really did...and probably still does...but that is a story for another day...), there was *The Unopened Files*: a very similar publication that Mark also edited, and which was also dedicated to the worlds of conspiracy and cover-up. I wrote quite a lot for *The Unopened Files*; including this article on Hollywood swashbuckler, babe-bagger extraordinaire, and all-round party-animal, Errol Flynn:

For people with a love and appreciation of cinematic history, the late actor, Errol Flynn, was the ultimate swashbuckling star of the 1940s. In movies such as *The Adventures of Robin Hood*, *Captain Blood*, *The Adventures of Don Juan*, and *The Charge of the Light Brigade*, Flynn earned his reputation as a force to be reckoned with in Hollywood, and became one of the most loved and admired screen stars of that bygone era. Behind the glossy, celluloid image that Flynn was careful to cultivate, however, there existed a far more intriguing, secret, and controversial persona.

From the previously classified files of numerous government, intelligence, and military agencies, comes a truly astonishing body of data on Flynn that covers such controversial issues as allegations of rape, extortion attempts, Hollywood scandal, and, most intriguing of all, links with both wartime Nazi spies and the Cold War-era activities of Cuba's Fidel Castro. It's no wonder that Flynn's FBI file alone runs to almost 400 pages.

Errol Leslie Thomson Flynn was born on June 20, 1909. He arrived in Hollywood in the early part of 1935, having traveled from Tasmania via New Guinea, London, and New York. Even at that stage, Flynn was embroiled in controversy: his departure from New Guinea, for example, was hastened by the fact that a warrant had been issued for his arrest on charges of illegally procuring native labour. He was twenty-six years of age and in the prime of his life. Not surprisingly, for someone thrust into the Hollywood lifestyle of fame, fortune, and glamour, Flynn lived life to the fullest: wine, women and adventure were the order of the day, both on- and off-screen.

At times, however, Flynn's adrenalin-driven lifestyle of non-stop parties, drugs, and booze went too far even for him. Declassified police records demonstrate that during the latter part of 1942, Flynn was accused of unlawful sexual intercourse with a striking seventeen-year-old blonde named Betty Hansen. According to Hansen, Flynn had raped her at the Bel Air home of one of his friends, Freddie McEvoy. Hansen's graphic testimony was presented in Los Angeles County Court on January 14, 1943, along with that of another girl, Peggy La Rue Satterlee, who was also alleging rape by Flynn. But records show that the allegations were summarily thrown out, and Flynn lived to fight another day. His problems, however, had barely begun.

It was during this period in his life and career that Flynn received the first of two extortion notes that found their way to the FBI's Technical Laboratory. The first note, sent only weeks after the rape controversy had died down, advised Flynn that if he "valued [his] life and career" he was to "send ten thousand dollars in cash wrapped in a small package" to a particular drop-off point, which was a malt shop in San Bernardino, California. Obviously concerned, Flynn contacted the authorities, and the declassified records show that the FBI made a detailed study of both the letter and its contents. Not only that: but FBI agents and local police initiated a stakeout of this malt shop.

As demanded by the extortion note, a package was duly left at the malt shop on the day in question, and the FBI patiently waited for its quarry to come along. All involved in the entrapment were utterly amazed, however, when the person turned out to be a thirteen-year-old boy named Billy Seamster. According to the FBI's files, young Billy was a fan of Flynn's and he maintained, rather weakly, that he had really only wanted the movie star's autograph. For their part, both the FBI and the police decided not to prosecute Billy because of his young age. In April 1943, Flynn received yet another extortion note. This time, however, it bore all of the hallmarks of something far more serious than a schoolboy prank:

> "MR FLYNN!!!! If you know what is good for you, you will pay attention to the girls you raped. I know you did it. You cannot fool me, so you better fork over some dough. Put your answer in the BOSTON DAILY RECORD. Put it near WEINCHELL [sic] column and just say anything but give a hint you received this and in a week if you don't want trouble. Get what I mean chum. Be hearing from you don't forget a week from today. That will be April 29 and then I will send you your instructions on where and when to leave the money and how much. Do not worry it will not be over $15,000 for that's all I need to skip town."

Again, the FBI launched an extensive investigation through the Bureau's Los Angeles office, with a wealth of assistance provided by FBI special agents in Boston, and by local police. Once more, the perpetrator was ultimately caught, and revealed this time to be one Robert Street, then on parole from the Medfield State Mental Hospital. But far worse things were to come for Flynn.

Additional official memoranda of 1943 show that during this same time frame, none other than FBI boss J. Edgar Hoover was out for Flynn's blood. Hoover wanted him charged under the White Slave Traffic Act because of a trip to Mexico Flynn had made with an 18-year-old girl named Nora Eddington (who would later become his wife) that Hoover and the FBI felt was not entirely innocent in nature. As the FBI stated in a wonderfully antiquated style on August 27, 1943: "The Bureau files maintain fragmentary information in connection with National Defense cases which attributed to Flynn a rather depraved character. Information in these files reflect that he is generally regarded in Hollywood circles as a 'wolf' who delights in achieving intimacies with young innocent girls."

Once again, however, the Teflon-like Flynn succeeded in escaping prosecution, as the following memorandum to FBI headquarters made clear: "Flynn and the girl have returned from Mexico: it is pretty much of a personal escapade and that [sic] the girl went to Mexico in company with Flynn with the consent of her parents."

Hollywood scandal was one thing, but darker allegations linked Flynn with something far more sinister: namely, deep connections to wartime Nazi spies. Flynn authority Charles Higham has stated: "I spoke to Colonel William E. Williamson, former director of demilitarization procedures in Japan under General [Douglas] MacArthur...Williamson had done his own research at the Pentagon and State Department and the CIA...and had learned that Errol was a spy for the Nazis on a major scale." Also, nightclub owner, and friend of Flynn's, Johnny Meyer told Higham: "I believe Errol was not merely in touch with the Nazis in San Francisco but was actively aiding and abetting them." And the alleged links do not end there.

It is a matter of official record that one of Flynn's girlfriends was Gertrude Anderson, a key Nazi agent who was the subject of deep FBI surveillance. According to Charles Higham, Flynn's friend Freddie McEvoy, at whose home Flynn was alleged to have raped Betty Hansen, had been under investigation as a possible collaborator with the Nazis. In the years leading up to the Second World War, she was involved in U-Boat refueling operations. Interestingly, the Government's files on Flynn include transcripts of telephone conversations between Flynn and McEvoy that were monitored by the wartime Office of Censorship.

Of particular note is a document that can be found within the Office of Censorship's files on Flynn that is dated December 14, 1942, and titled *American Film Actor Reported Associating With German Agent In Mexico*. This document details the testimony of an unnamed informant who had provided the Office with some intriguing material:

> "Writer, after telling of three weeks spent in Acapulco...adds, Errol Flynn came up to the hotel for drinks a couple of evenings bringing his girl along –

> Hilda Kruger, leading German spy here, arranged the date for him. An associate of hers, another Nazi suspect, gave Errol Flynn and Frederik McEvoy as references while spending time in California."

Most controversial of all, however, was Flynn's friendship with a certain Dr. Hermann Frederick Erben. Born on November 15, 1897, in Vienna, Austria, Erben was described in Lionel Godfrey's *The Life and Crimes of Errol Flynn*, as "a specialist in tropical diseases." Indeed, he was. However, he was much more, according to Flynn authority Charles Higham, who described Erben as "one of the most important and ingenious Nazi agents."

Erben had graduated from the State High School, Vienna, in 1915, and between that year and 1918 had served with the Austrian Army, before being honorably discharged as a First Lieutenant. Eight years later, Erben received a fellowship to study in the United States, and while there was granted an Immigration Visa. In 1927 he was licensed to practice medicine and surgery in Louisiana, and the following year was he was also licensed for the state of Washington. But what of Erben's friendship with Flynn? The files of the Intelligence Detachment Screening Center make for eye-opening reading:

> "1932: [Erben] went via the Far East to New Guinea on another scientific expedition, which was financed by himself. On this trip he met the film star Errol Flynn and became a very close friend of same. 1937: [Erben] returned from South America and in the same year he and his friend Errol Flynn embarked in New York for London and went via Paris. Being in London [Erben] volunteered with a British ambulance unit, which was committed for the loyalists in Spain. Errol Flynn also went as a journalist and unofficial observer to Spain. After 20 days in Spain, subject went to Vienna and from there to Canton, China."

Erben had a darker side, too. American authorities were able to confirm that he *had* worked as a Nazi agent during the Second World War. Details of this startling fact can be found within the files of the Intelligence Detachment Screening Centre, and specifically in the pages of a document titled *Subject Accepted The Job As German Intelligence Agent*:

> "[Erben] claims that he accepted the proposition to become a German intelligence agent, fully conscious of the fact that at the present, he was still an American citizen, and thus subject to the penalty of high treason. [Erben] admits that he was not forced or coerced to accept the job."

Needless to say, because of his close friendship with Erben, Flynn was interviewed by FBI agents who subsequently prepared a two-page report, from which the following is extracted:

> "Mr. FLYNN at the outset of the interview, admitted being acquainted with Dr ERBEN and regarded him highly. They have been acquainted for about ten years and have traveled extensively together all over the world. Mr. FLYNN stated that heretofore ERBEN had been very much opposed to Nazism and communism and from what he, FLYNN, knows of his background,

he does not believe ERBEN would now be a devout Nazi."

The FBI and the IDSC were not the only ones watching the activities of Flynn and Erben. The wartime Office of Strategic Services, a precursor to the CIA, was doing likewise. The OSS stated starkly in its files on the men that "Erben tried to return to the United States as a repatriate. We believe that if he had been successful in so doing, he would have been acting in the United States as an agent of the German government. Erben's only contact in the United States was Errol Flynn. We know of absolutely no other contact with Dr Erben there."

Flynn authority Charles Higham uncovered data suggesting that the British Government had intriguing files on Flynn, too. In Higham's own words: "In early 1980, I was interviewed about Flynn for an American radio program. One of the callers who took part was a woman called Anne Lane…she said that she had worked from 1946 to 1951 for the MI5 chief Sir Percy Sillitoe…Lane had been in charge of the Flynn dossier, which she described clearly as a beige, red-ribboned [sic] concertina file stamped MOST SECRET.

"The file," added Higham,

> "revealed that Flynn had been under surveillance by both MI5 and MI6 since 1934, when he made pro-Nazi remarks at a party in Mayfair. Flynn had also been monitored by British intelligence at a Paris meeting in 1937 with high-ranking German officials and the Duke of Windsor, a meeting clearly inimical to British interests…SIS [The Special Intelligence Service] also traced him to the security area at Berchtesgaden in the spring of 1938, where (according to sworn statements by Erben in 1946, made to a British security officer) he had a secret meeting with Hitler."

So much for Flynn's still-unresolved and decidedly mysterious wartime activities: but what of the final years of the man's life? Declassified files from the late 1950s that originated with the State Department, tell an intriguing story. By now, Flynn's roller-coaster lifestyle had completely and utterly ravaged his once healthy, athletic body. The heartthrob-star of the late 1930s and 1940s had, by the 1950s, become a pathetic shadow of his former self. Racked with illness, a drug- and alcohol-dependent Flynn had lost his position as the number one Hollywood box office draw but not his uncanny knack for attracting controversy at an official level.

In 1959, the State Department recorded the details of its surveillance of Flynn's activities while he was on the island of Cuba:

> "Fidel Castro has asked Errol Flynn, movie actor, to suggest someone who might be able to take over the Sans Souci gambling casino…Flynn is modestly displaying a minor leg wound these days which he says was inflicted by government bullets while he was roving with a rebel band last week. Flynn told a press conference here that he had been out three times since Christmas with rebel raiders in the service of Fidel Castro, whom he has known for eight years."

Only months later, Flynn's past finally caught up with him. On October 14, 1959, he died of a heart attack in Vancouver, Canada, at the all-too-young age of fifty. According to the coroner's report, Flynn's death was attributed to "coronary thrombosis of the arteries, degeneration of the liver and infection of the lower intestines."

Despite the fact that the many and varied files declassified by the FBI, the State Department, the Office of Strategic Services, the Office of Censorship, and the Intelligence Detachment Screening Center all throw intriguing light on Flynn's career, his wild-times, his links with Nazi spies, his time spent covering the Spanish Civil War, his connections to Fidel Castro, and much more, it is fair to say that in some ways those same files, fragmentary as they are when it comes to stating with certainty that Flynn was in league with the Nazis, only serve to deepen the mystery of his truly extraordinary private life. Errol Flynn was, without doubt, enigmatic to the very end.

Unconventional Aircraft 1998

Back in 1998, I freely admit, I was still in full-on 'I want to believe' mode: Mulder could do no wrong, there were dead aliens under RAF Rudloe Manor, and the truth was, of course, out there. And, perhaps, no article better summed up my mind-set back then this one (titled *Unconventional Aircraft*), which I penned for the brothers-Birdsall, and which had many a rabid conspiracy theorist overjoyed:

Until now it has generally been believed that, aside from a few sporadic UFO investigations, the British Government did not become seriously concerned by the UFO mystery until September 1952, when multiple UFO encounters were reported over the North Sea and the mainland during the course of a NATO exercise codenamed *Mainbrace*. Records available at the Public Record Office and at the National Archives in the USA, reveal that numerous UFO reports were filed by RAF and U.S. Air Force personnel who had seen unusual, circular-shaped vehicles manoeuvring over strategic airfields and over the USS *Franklin D. Roosevelt* aircraft carrier during the exercise. As a result, in the months that followed, at least one division of the Air Ministry established a project to try and determine the truth that lay behind the *Mainbrace* - and similar - events.

This scenario was bolstered further by the words of the late Ralph Noyes, who was involved in UFO investigations whilst working with the Ministry of Defence in the 1960s and 1970s. According to Noyes: 'I reached a fairly senior grade in the MoD and had access to whatever documents were necessary to my responsibilities. These included TOP SECRET material generally, as well as many other papers of a still-restricted character. The Air Staff, in 1950 to 1952, were taking only the most perfunctory (and embarrassed) cognisance of "saucer stories".'

Moreover, commenting on the UFO encounters reported during *Mainbrace* in September 1952, Noyes asserted that:

> 'No folder, still less an official file, had yet been opened by the Operations staff on flying saucers. Whether or not that was a dereliction of duty I leave to others.'

While Noyes *did* prove to be a valuable source of data on matters pertaining to official British Government policy on the UFO subject, it can now be argued with a high-degree of certainty that he was not in possession of the full facts. It was in 1999 that I was able to secure from the Public Record Office a copy of a lengthy file (title *Unorthodox Aircraft*) that now gives us an illuminating insight into previously-unknown government involvement in the UFO subject.

The newly surfaced file itself is of interest and significance for a number of reasons. First, much of the material contained within it was classified at *Secret* level (with a considerable number of papers stamped *Top Secret*). Second, the file makes it very clear that the Air Ministry was not the only department involved in the UFO subject during the late 1940s. And third, there is evidence to show that, at the time, the British Government was monitoring the UFO subject on what was quite literally a global scale.

It should be noted that much of the file focuses on the analysis of radical and new (for the time, of course) secret aircraft designs perfected by the-then Soviet Union. Given the fact that in the late 1940s the Soviets were becoming a major world threat, this is perfectly understandable. And as the file also makes clear, detailed studies were undertaken by British Air Intelligence in an attempt to determine the extent to which the Soviets had made advances in both rocket and jet propulsion. Interestingly, the file shows that Air Intelligence conducted a large number of interviews in the period 1948-50 with former wartime prisoners of war, who were held on military camps in Russia and who might have viewed the results of secret aircraft trials undertaken by the Soviets in the immediate post-war era.

Moreover, the results of Air Intelligence's investigations were forwarded for analysis to a veritable host of departments and agencies within the British Government and military. This would routinely include (a) the head of the Joint Intelligence Bureau at Bryanston Square, London; (b) the director of the Air Ministry's Scientific and Technical Intelligence Branch (STIB); (c) several key intelligence divisions in the Royal Air Force; and (d) MI10 at the War Office. Most astonishing of all, also contained within the *Unconventional Aircraft* file are a host of papers pertaining to UFOs – all of which were circulated to the aforementioned departments.

With respect to unidentified flying objects, what, precisely, does the relevant paperwork tell us? In the period 1948-1949, sources within the British Government were extremely interested in determining the extent to which the Nazis had succeeded in constructing flying saucer-like aircraft during the Second World War; and furthermore, those same sources were expressing concern regarding the extent to which the Soviets might have capitalised on this technology in the post-war era. (This may, of course, be due to the fact that there was a belief in many quarters – and demonstrated in the files acquired by Andy Roberts and Dr. David Clarke - that the Nazis were responsible for the *Foo Fighter* phenomenon.)

This can be amply shown by virtue of the fact that as far back as September 1949, the Air Ministry's Scientific and Technical Intelligence Branch was regularly receiving clippings culled from all manner of publications on both Nazi saucers and various other UFO reports. To illustrate this, on 14 September 1949, the STIB received from the Press Information Room of the Air Ministry's Intelligence Division, a selection of newspaper reports concerning UFO activity over Vienna, Austria. *Now it's Flaming Saucers*, proclaimed one such clipping from the *Daily Herald* on 12 September 1949.

Similarly, only months later, the STIB received from the Press Information Room, a large batch of magazine articles photocopied from German newspapers and science periodicals on both highly-advanced flying saucer designs postulated by the Nazis during the Second World War, as well as post-War designs on the drawing-boards of the Soviets and the Americans. But there is more.

Those sources within the JIB, the Air Ministry, STIB and MI10 who were regularly receiving such material from at least 1949 onwards, also took note of two matters that, historically speaking, are now an established part of UFO lore. Of those who in the 1950s, 60s and 70s openly accused the American Government of conspiring to hide the truth surrounding the UFO problem from the general public, perhaps the most vocal was Major Donald Keyhoe. A graduate of the U.S. Naval Academy and a former pilot with the Marine Corps, Keyhoe went on to write five highly controversial books that chronicled his UFO investigations – the first, titled *The Flying Saucers Are Real* was published in 1950. In 1949, however, Keyhoe had written a now-historic article for the U.S. magazine *True* that detailed his findings and thoughts on the UFO subject. According to a *True* write-up of Keyhoe's article: 'This is the most interesting and important true story we have ever published. It is utterly true. We can document every occurrence reported here. It is our sober, considered conviction that the conclusion arrived at in this story is a fact, that…The Flying Saucers Are Real.'

In his 1950 book, *The Flying Saucers Are Real*, Keyhoe recalled the effect that the publication of the *True* article had in official U.S. circles. 'The publicity was far more than I had expected. I phoned up a reporter in Washington whose beat includes the Pentagon. "The Air Force is running around in circles," he told me. "They knew your story was due, but nobody thought it would raise such a fuss. I think they're scared of hysteria. They're getting a barrage of wires and telephone calls. They're going to deny the whole thing. But I heard one Press Branch guy say it might not be enough – they're trying to figure some way to knock it down fast."'

In other words, Keyhoe's article – that concluded UFOs were very possibly 'interplanetary spacecraft' – was causing major repercussions on the part of the U.S. Government. It is, therefore, highly illuminating to note that a copy of Keyhoe's article features prominently in the British Government's *Unorthodox Aircraft* file too. Moreover, a copy found its way to *all* of the aforementioned British government and military departments. Evidently, it was not just the Americans who were concerned by Keyhoe's disclosures.

In addition to the Keyhoe article, the Air Ministry's Scientific and Technical Intelligence Branch also took a keen interest in the now famous series of photographs taken by a farmer named Paul Trent at McMinnville, Oregon, USA, on 11 May 1950. And again, the data received a wide distribution throughout the British Government's intelligence community. Of all the many and varied photographs of UFOs that have been taken since 1947, it is notable that the Air Ministry should have been so intrigued by the Trent pictures. Consider the following extract from an official U.S. report on Trent's experience. 'This is one of the few UFO reports in which all factors investigated, geometric, psychological and physical, appear to be consistent with the assertion that an extraordinary flying object, silvery, metallic, disk-shaped, tens of meters in diameter, and evidently artificial, flew within sight of the two witnesses.'

It is also worth noting that in a newspaper clipping contained within one of the *Unorthodox Aircraft* file entries, Air Chief Marshal Sir Philip Joubert commented that: 'The object pictured is very odd, and it is impossible even to guess what it is. It is clearly not a meteorite. Therefore, it is either a machined or cast structure. It shows no sign of any method of propulsion. It looks like a "skimming dish" – except for that little stump at the top, which in both pictures is at the same angle.' Perhaps most eye-opening, is Joubert's comment that: *'We have had at least thirty instances of this sort of object being seen.'* Note also that Joubert – a British Air Chief Marshal – very clearly stated *'we'* as opposed to the Americans.

Also contained within the *Unorthodox Aircraft* file are a series of enclosures that may have a bearing on an altogether far more serious and controversial matter. In the latter part of 1998, it was revealed that an American UFO researcher named Timothy Cooper had obtained a series of documents that allegedly originated with a super-secret agency buried in the heart of the U.S. intelligence community and known as *Majestic 12*. Supposedly, the organisation (which is also referred to as *MJ12* and *Majic 12*) was created in 1947 by the then U.S. president, Harry Truman, in response to the covert retrieval of a crashed UFO and alien bodies at Roswell, New Mexico, and was comprised of leading scientists, intelligence and military personnel.

Needless to say, opinion is sharply divided as to whether these papers are the genuine article (Cooper asserts that they were supplied to him by an inside source) or some form of sophisticated hoax. At the time of writing and despite numerous investigations and studies of the documents, no concrete conclusions regarding their veracity (or otherwise) have been reached. However, the *Unconventional Aircraft* file contains a number of entries that tie together two subjects that have a direct bearing on the *Majestic 12* papers and that, normally, one would imagine would have no connection whatsoever – namely UFOs and bacteriological warfare operations. Consider first the following extracts from the *Majestic 12* documents that refer to the unexplained deaths of a number of *MJ12*-connected personnel who allegedly came into contact with alien bodies found at Roswell:

> 'The panel was concerned over the contamination of several personnel

upon coming in contact with debris near the power plant [of the UFO]. One technician was overcome and collapsed when he attempted the removal of the body. Another medical technician went into a coma four hours after placing a body in a rubber body bag. All four later died of seizures and profuse bleeding. All four were wearing protective suits when they came in contact with body fluids from the occupants.'

The documentation continues:

'*BIOLOGCAL WARFARE PROGRAMS*: BW programs in U.S. and U.K. are in field test stages. Discovery of new virus and bacteria agents so lethal, that serums derived by genetic research, can launch medical science into unheard of fields of biology. The samples extracted from bodies found in New Mexico, have yielded new strains of a retrovirus not totally understood, but give promise of the ultimate BW weapon. The danger lies in the spread of airborne and blood borne outbreaks of diseases in large populations, with no medical cures available.'

As I stated above, thus far the provenance of these particular papers has not been determined. However, these particular sections of the papers have led the father-son team of UFO researchers Robert and Ryan Wood to comment that: 'this was the early 50s and biological weapons were just getting into early swing in the UK and US. They were having great insight from these alien bodies, trying to better understand these humanoid creatures. What they did is to create a few strains of retrovirus that were not totally understood from the aliens. That provided promise for the greatest biological weapon of all time.'

Of course, if the governments of both Britain and the USA *have* succeeded in creating the ultimate biological warfare weapon from alien-derived DNA, then this would be a matter of profound significance. However, the problem is that absolutely nothing has surfaced officially to link together the two issues of UFOs and biological warfare. Until now.

When I first received the *Unorthodox Aircraft* papers from the PRO, I was astonished to learn that in precisely the same time frame referenced in the *Majestic 12* documents, the Air Ministry's Intelligence Division was regularly forwarding classified data to the Directorate of Scientific Intelligence at the Metropole Buildings, London, on two subjects: UFOs and bacteriological warfare. Moreover, these documents were declassified officially in the U.K. only months after Timothy Cooper received (in an unofficial capacity) the leaked *Majestic 12* files.

I quote from one of the entries (picked entirely at random) from the Public Record Office-originated material: 'Subject: Bacteriological Warfare Article. Forwarded herewith is a further instalment of a series of articles at present appearing in the publication "*Kristall*" by Dr. Stubenbauer. Your attention is also drawn to the article on "Flying Saucers" appearing in the same publication.'

Although only brief in nature, this uniquely important paper (that, recall, has been declassified officially by the British Government – it is *not* a leaked paper of questionable provenance) links in the same breath 'bacteriological warfare' and 'flying saucers'. Moreover, the department that received the report (of which the above is simply one of many) was none other than the Directorate of Scientific Intelligence at the Metropole Buildings. This is of profound interest for two reasons. First, in 1990, the PRO informed me that a number of DSI files were at that time still classified for one hundred years. And second, according to retired intelligence officer, Gordon Creighton, who himself worked at the Metropole Buildings at the time in question: 'I was on the next floor to the department that dealt with UFOs...There weren't any other departments on that floor. But I and one or two other people in my department used to have fun when we were going up or down in the lift with a bunch of these chaps, talking about UFOs!'

This is not the first time that allegations have surfaced in the U.K. linking UFOs, alien bodies and bacteriological warfare under one, unified banner. In 1996, retired British police sergeant Tony Dodd stated that he had interviewed a former British Army source that claimed to have transported alien bodies in 1974 to the Government's Chemical and Biological Defence Establishment at Porton Down, Wiltshire.

Oddly enough, only months after the *Unorthodox Aircraft* file surfaced into the public domain, Nick Pope (a former UFO investigator at the Ministry of Defence) wrote a novel titled *Operation Thunderchild* that revolved around a hostile attack on the United Kingdom by alien forces. At the time, stories and rumours were in circulation to the effect that Pope was telling in a fictionalised format, 'the truth' that he was unable to reveal in a non-fiction book. Regardless of whether or not this is the case, in *Operation Thunderchild*, alien bodies recovered from a UFO crash are taken to the Chemical and Biological Defence Establishment at Porton Down.

When *Operation Thunderchild* was published, I questioned Nick Pope vigorously regarding the claims that the book was base more on fact than fiction. His comments are illuminating, to say the least. 'Even to you, Nick, I can't comment on that. But let's put it this way: *Operation Thunderchild* is going to be more controversial than *Open Skies, Closed Minds* or *The Uninvited* [Author's note: Pope's previous non-fiction titles]; and, indeed, the Ministry of Defence may have more of a problem with it. Mainly because it's going to feature real locations, real weapon systems, real tactics, real doctrine and real crisis management techniques. It's going to blend my knowledge and experience of UFOs with my knowledge of crisis management – such as my involvement in the Gulf War where I worked in the Joint Operations Centre.'

> 'Given that you won't comment on the hypothesis that *Operation Thunderchild* relates in a fictional format the sorts of things that you were legally unable to relate in a non-fiction book, are you saying that there is more going on behind the scenes than meets the eye?'

I asked Pope.

Positively oozing uneasiness, he replied:

> 'Well, it's very difficult to go into the details, but I'm a bit more inclined to

think that there's perhaps more to this than meets the eye.'

I continued: 'More to what?'

'I...er...there are, um, one or two things about the Ministry's stance over the last few years that have caused me to question things perhaps a little bit more than I did previously. I do think that there's a little bit more going on than perhaps I previously thought. I have to be very careful with every single word I say, because I know that every sentence, every nuance, will be scrutinized by the MoD and *a number of other agencies.*'

'Excuse me, Nick: a number of other agencies? What do you mean by that?' I pressed.

'I mean, a number of other agencies,' was his tight-lipped reply.

Try as I might, I could not get Nick Pope to expand on this most curious statement. However, at the same time that the PRO was declassifying files on UFOs and biological warfare, leaked documents were surfacing in the USA and Nick Pope's *Operation Thunderchild* was released, the Ministry of Defence, in an unprecedented move, gave a huge amount of technical assistance and support to a BBC TV production titled *Invasion Earth* that dealt with an attack on the planet by hostile aliens.

Inevitably, this led to theories that this was all part of a less-than-subtle attempt on the part of the MoD to get the general public thinking about the possibility of humankind waging war with an alien species. Does the MoD know something that we don't? An MoD source referred to me by Nick Pope had a number of perceptive comments to make. 'It's extremely strange,' he began, 'that on the one hand the MoD is publicly so dismissive about UFOs; and yet on the other it bent over backwards to provide assistance to a TV company producing a science-fiction drama which starts with the RAF shooting down a UFO.

'Normally,' he continued,

'the Ministry of Defence only helps film and TV companies where it believes that significant benefits will fall to the MoD in terms of recruiting, training or public relations. This was the case, for example, with our participation in *Soldier, Soldier* and in the *James Bond* film, *Tomorrow Never Dies*. What, one wonders, did the MoD think it had to gain from helping to perpetuate a view that the Royal Air Force were virtually at war with extra-terrestrials? Questions about our participation in this project were raised at the highest level within the Ministry of Defence.'

Before I turn to other matters, three months after the *Unorthodox Aircraft* files surfaced, I was given an original edition of a NASA paper titled CONCEPTS FOR DETECTION OF EXTRATERRESTRIAL LIFE. Although utterly genuine, the document was not released officially. Rather, it was, to put things diplomatically, 'liberated' from a certain archive. The document had been sent to the A.V. Roe aircraft company at Manchester (and specifically to its Weapons Research Division) by NASA. Here, then, is yet another example of official files making a link between extra-terrestrial life and weapons research.

With the essence of the *Unorthodox Aircraft* documentation now largely detailed, let us try and come to a few conclusions. The file highlights graphically the fact that certain elements of the Air Ministry were interested in the issue of secret UFO-like technology developed by Nazi Germany and the Soviet Union. That same material was circulated amongst a host of departments, including the Joint Intelligence Bureau, MI10 and the Directorate of Scientific Intelligence. And finally, senior and key figures within the DSI were – as far back as 1950 – receiving classified briefings on both UFOs and biological weapons research. This, of course, raises important questions. Is it merely down to chance that in precisely the same time frame that unofficial papers surfaced in the USA linking the exploitation of the bodies allegedly recovered at Roswell in 1947 with biological warfare operations, officially released papers referencing both UFOs and bio-warfare should have been declassified in the U.K.? Is this an indication of a '*drip-feed*' operation on the part of sources within both the American and British intelligence services?

Whatever the ultimate answers to those questions, in April 2000, the Public Record Office released a second volume of documentation titled *Unorthodox Aircraft* that covered the period 1950-1952. Again, the contents of the file were focused on UFOs, newspaper and magazine articles on unidentified aerial phenomena and so-called Nazi Flying Saucers. What sets this latest release of files apart from any other UFO-related documents declassified into the public domain by officialdom is the cover page.

Classified *Top Secret*, at the top of the page the following words appear: 'THE TITLE OF THIS FILE MUST NOT APPEAR ON THE OUTER COVER.' And at the foot of the document, this is followed by: 'TO BE KEPT UNDER LOCK AND KEY.'

I have had the opportunity to examine literally thousands of pages of formerly classified files on UFOs at the Public Record Office. Never before, however, have I come across a UFO-related file that was deemed so sensitive by officialdom that its contents were to be kept under lock and key at all times. In 1991, in his book *Alien Liaison*, Timothy Good, related the testimony of a former counter-intelligence investigator who had learned that in the mid-1960s, files on UFOs were held at the RAF's Flying Complaints Flight office at Government Buildings, Bromyard Avenue, Acton.

According to Good's source,

> 'I had access to every *Top Secret* file there was, except Low Flying, because I understand they dealt with UFOs,' said the investigator. 'We could get in anywhere, but not in that department. I remember they used to have an Air Ministry guard in the passage – you couldn't get past them. We could see the Provost Marshal's top secret files but yet I couldn't get into the place dealing

with UFOs.'

Good's source further elaborated that the location of this material was 'a well-locked office at the end of a corridor'.

At the time that Good's book was released, I spoke with a well-known British UFO investigator who stated that it was absurd to believe that the British military had in its possession *any* UFO data that had to be kept 'locked away'. With the release of the latest batch of *Unconventional Aircraft* papers, however, it can be safely said that the British Government *was* in possession of UFO data that it determined had to be kept under lock and key at all times – and at least half a century ago.

When the above-documentation surfaced into the public domain in early 2000, several people commented that it is common practice for *all Top Secret* documents to be subjected to such stringent security. I do not dispute this. However, according to officialdom, the UFO subject is one that has *never* had a bearing on national security. Moreover, the MoD asserts that *all* of its UFO files are unclassified in nature. Unfortunately, the MoD's stance is totally negated by the release of papers such as those cited above. There are, therefore, but two possibilities. Either the UFO controversy was (and still is) considered highly sensitive by U.K. authorities (and this is why such tight security was applied); or trained and experienced MoD personnel in the late 1940s and early 1950s were applying totally unwarranted security constraints to trivial and unclassified material. To accept the latter is, I believe, beyond the bounds of credibility.

The Ministry of Defence.

Banned - The BBC and the Bomb 1999

I wrote several more articles for Mark Birdsall's *The Unopened Files* in 1999, including the following one, *Banned: The BBC and the Bomb*; a dark and disturbing story of nuclear-war, four-minute warnings, public fear and anxiety, high-level chicanery, and the behind-closed-doors world of good old 'Auntie Beeb':

It is seldom that the on-screen worlds of sci-fi and reality are successfully blended in such a way that they attract the attention and concern of the highest echelons of Government. But such a scenario is by no means unknown. A perfect example was a British TV sci-fi production called *The War Game*. Produced in 1965 by Peter Watkins for the British Broadcasting Corporation (BBC), *The War Game* painted a horrific, futuristic picture of what life would be like in Britain in the event of a global, thermonuclear war: atomic devastation, death on a truly massive scale, widespread radiation poisoning, disease, starvation, mercy killings at the hands of the military for irradiated members of the public, firing squads for looters – presuming, of course, that there was anyone in an official position left alive to order the firing squads – and the total breakdown of society.

Whereas Hollywood's 1983 sci-fi drama on nuclear war, *The Day After*, produced lasting images of hope for the masses - to the effect that humanity would ultimately surface from the ashes and all would one day be well - *The War Game* did precisely the opposite. Its bleak message was that following a complete nuclear exchange between the super-powers of the Cold War, those who survived the initial holocaust and the inevitable complete and utter breakdown of society and civilization that was destined to follow, would be faced with a future so terrible, and from which widespread recovery would be an undoubted impossibility, that instant death in the atomic inferno would seem like a blessing.

Today, decades after it was made, *The War Game* has lost none of its stark impact. Despite the fact that the show was produced in 1965, it was never shown on British television until 1985 – the same year that the BBC broadcast an even more unsettling and graphic drama on nuclear war titled *Threads*. But why would the BBC ban a drama that combined in such a unique fashion the world of science fact and sci-fi? Was it simply a unilateral decision of the BBC to spare the population at large the horrific reality of a nuclear war that might never happen, anyway? To answer those questions, it becomes necessary to examine a formerly classified British Government file that remained classified for decades.

It was in 1963 that Peter Watkins first put forward a proposal to the BBC for *The War Game* – a proposal that would graphically, and specifically, illustrate the effects of a nuclear attack on the British county of Kent. Despite the controversial nature of Watkins' idea, it *was* accepted by the BBC that stated: "So long as there is no security risk, and the facts are authentic, the people should be trusted with the truth." Nevertheless, "the people" were *not* given the facts.

In November 1965, and with the production of *The War Game* complete, the then-director-general of the BBC, Hugh Greene, arrogantly announced that the program would not be broadcast: "This is the BBC's own decision. It has been taken after a good deal if thought and discussion but not as a result of outside pressure of any kind." A condescending Greene continued that *The War Game* was, "too horrifying for the medium of broadcasting." As a result, for two decades both the film and its apocalyptic message lay buried in the darkened vaults of the BBC.

While it is true that the ultimate decision not to broadcast Peter Watkins' show was the BBC's, as Duncan Campbell noted in his chilling book *War Plan UK*, "outside pressure" had indeed been brought to bear on the BBC. As Campbell stated: "Late in September [1965] a party of Whitehall's highest visited the Television Center, unannounced." That party, Campbell added, consisted of the British Government's Cabinet Secretary, Sir Burke Trend; Home Office Permanent Under-Secretary, Sir Charles Cunningham; officials from the Ministry of Defense; and the Defense Chiefs of Staff. The Government was unanimous: it was not in what was patronizingly termed the "public interest" for *The War Game* to be broadcast, and a blanket ban at the hands of the BBC was the order of the day. Now-declassified, official files reveal, however, that the seeds of the Government's decision to bring pressure to bear on the BBC to ensure that the film was not shown to the masses had, in fact, been sown as far back as at least 1954.

"I am informed that the BBC are proposing to broadcast in the New Year a program on the Hydrogen bomb," wrote the Prime Minister Winston Churchill in a personal minute to the minister responsible for the BBC, Earl De La Warr, on 17 December 1954. Churchill continued:

> "I doubt whether it is wise that they should do this. And I am sure that Ministers should see the script in advance, in order to satisfy themselves

that it contains nothing which is contrary to the public interest."

As a result of Churchill's desire to try and influence the BBC, immediate steps were taken on the part of the Government to determine the extent of the BBC's proposed plans: within twenty-four hours a battery of questions were fired at the BBC: What did the Corporation intend to broadcast? What information on thermonuclear weapons would be contained in the program? And, as with *The War Game*, would such a production be in the public interest? The Government demanded answers.

For its part, the BBC flatly denied that any firm plans had been initiated for such a program, but did admit that ideas had been mooted by "one of our producers." Despite the BBC's assurances that at that stage nothing concrete had been decided, behind the closed doors of the official world, concern was mounting fast. An extract from a four-page report of January 7, 1955 stamped *Highly Confidential* and titled *Government "Interference" with BBC Program* stated:

> "It would be quite wrong to have programs on this subject which tended to persuade the public in the U.K. that there was no point in trying to defend themselves against such an all-destructive weapon."

Additional documentation contained within the file reiterates this point and makes it very clear that the Government's prime concern was not so much the fact that the BBC was contemplating the broadcast of a program on the Hydrogen Bomb per se. Rather, the major area of worry was whether or not any proposed show would reveal the devastating effects that a nuclear attack would have on the population of Great Britain. For example, a *Secret* memo of February 15, 1955 contained within the file and that dealt with official, nuclear policy, stated: "The aim of the Government would be to avoid giving such a pessimistic picture that the public would feel 'what is the use of doing anything?'"

Perhaps most astonishing of all, however, is an entry in the document collection that refers, in apparent seriousness, to the Government's sincere hope that in the event of a nuclear war – with an official forecast of tens of millions likely to be killed in Britain alone in the initial bombing, and millions more dying in the immediate aftermath from the effects of radiation, burns, starvation, disease and bomb-blast - there would be a "resolute determination" on the part of population to "see the thing through whatever befall." Needless to say, such comments defy belief.

It is also interesting to note that the British were very possibly following a lead set down by their American cousins. A *Secret* report contained in the file reveals:

> "Up to the present the United States Government were compelled by their existing law to be very secretive about thermonuclear bombs and they had given us little or no information on the effects produced by the bomb. It was only recently that we were able to get such information from our own experiments. Nevertheless, we had been in the closest touch with the United States Government as to how the matter should be presented to the public."

It is not surprising that British authorities did not wish to see the effects of a nuclear attack made available to the public by the BBC: in the same year that Prime Minister Winston Churchill expressed concern over the BBC's proposals, President Dwight D. Eisenhower's Technological Capabilities Panel of the Scientific Advisory Committee published a report titled *Meeting the Threat of Surprise Attack*, that outlined one particularly bleak scenario that would follow a major nuclear strike by the Soviet Union on the continental United States. In part, the document stated:

> "A surface blast 10 Megaton bomb can result in covering an area of 2500-5000 square miles with sufficient activity that a person in the open for one day immediately following detonation will receive a dose large enough to cause radiation sickness; an area of 700 to 1400 square miles would receive sufficient activity to cause death to most people who are similarly exposed."

Doubtless, some of this information would have filtered back to Winston Churchill, hence his Government's policy of keeping the BBC and the public ignorant and away from the controversy surrounding nuclear war. Meanwhile, another entry in the file makes much the same point:

> "The Government's main anxiety was that they should retain control over the manner in which the effects of nuclear weapons were made known to the public. Great care would be needed in striking the right note, so that the public were made aware of the full power of these weapons without being led thereby to adopt an attitude either of despair or of indifference to the need for effective measures of defence."

Notably a memo of February 16, 1955 asserted that the BBC had come to a decision by that date that:

> "It was unlikely that the BBC would wish to mount any feature program on 'fall out' or other effects of nuclear weapons but, if at any time they thought of doing so, they would certainly proceed in consultation with the Ministry of Defence."

It was this statement that led Churchill to maintain that the BBC had "willingly accepted" the Government's position, when in reality and behind closed doors, the BBC was vehemently against any such form of Government censorship.

Nevertheless, thus was laid down the unofficial and uneasy policy between the BBC and the Government that ultimately relegated *The War Game* to its twenty-year burial behind the closed doors of the BBC. Indeed, it was this same policy that gave the Government of the day a profound sense of relief. For example, extracts from the file show that to some officials, the idea of officially banning the BBC from producing a TV sci-fi drama on nuclear war was perceived as a highly fraught move. One unnamed official said: "The Government must have the right to indicate to the BBC where it felt the Corporation might be stepping beyond the bounds of international safety, yet the independence of the BBC from Government control was a vital matter."

In an age that has seen the fall of the Berlin Wall and the collapse of the Soviet Union, it might seem irrelevant to be discussing decades-old official documents on a TV sci-fi drama on the subject of nuclear war. However, both *The War Game* and the papers in question address bigger issues in our lives: they deal with the public's right to know; of the ability of the media to freely - and without government interference and surveillance of the type demonstrated above – inform that same public on matters of critical concern; and the fine line that exists between what should remain withheld in the interests of national security and that which some dark-suited official figure has deemed is not in the "public interest."

Another Gig, Another Planet 1999/2000

Yes, I know: a terrible, awful pun on the *Only Ones* classic song, *Another Girl, Another Planet*, but one that is highly apt for this particular section of the book. One afternoon, in late '99, I got a phone call from a certain Cyril Hards, a man running a company in the Midlands town of Solihull that was then in the ambitious process of establishing a new Sunday newspaper to be titled *The Planet on Sunday* – and, guess what, Clark Kent was nowhere in sight! A question was quickly posed to me: was I interested in writing a weekly column for the *PoS* on UFOs? I most assuredly was. And: I most assuredly did. At least: until *The Planet* folded after about two months of poor sales. Sadly, I saw the inevitable end coming from practically day-one. But, freelancing is a hostile, cut-throat world; and so I grabbed the veritable bull (or pounds and pennies) by the horns for as long as was conceivably possible. And here are a few selections from my time as cub-reporter for *The Planet on Sunday*:

A Cosmic Conspiracy

For years it has been assumed by UFO investigators that if the British Government has in its possession secret information pertaining to UFOs, that it does not wish to share with the populace at large, that those secrets are largely held by the Ministry of Defence and the Royal Air Force.

However, thanks to the industrious research of a spirited UFO researcher named Robin Cole, a fascinating body of data has surfaced linking the highly secret Government Communications Headquarters (GCHQ) at Cheltenham with the UFO mystery.

Created only twelve months after the Allied victory over the Nazis in the Second World War, GCHQ has the daunting task of supplying numerous agencies and departments within both Government and the military with intelligence data. It is also involved in various foreign and domestic eavesdropping operations – including the monitoring of emails, faxes and telephone conversations.

Born and bred in Cheltenham, Robin Cole has been fascinated by UFOs since childhood and, in the latter part of 1996, found himself plunged into the murky world of GCHQ, following a spectacular series of UFO incidents that occurred off the east coast of England.

It was shortly after 3.00 a.m. on 5 October 1996 when all hell broke loose in the skies over Norfolk and Suffolk. Multiple objects of unknown origin manifested themselves in British airspace, and, what's more, they were seen by credible sources, including serving police officers. They were tracked on ground-based military radar and were viewed out at sea by the crew of a tanker named the *Conocoast*.

'We can see a strange red-and-green rotating light in the sky directly south-east from Skegness,' reported police on the East coast, continuing: 'It looks strange as it is stationary and there is [sic] no aircraft in the area.' Equally unusual things were afoot at RAF Neatishead, Norfolk, as the following statement made to the Coast Guard by staff at Neatishead makes amply clear: 'We had a report from [RAF] Northwood that a civil flight had also reported strange lights in the area. They fit exactly what was seen from the ground: multi-coloured, flashing, stationary lights.'

For its part, the Government was very quick indeed to play down the events in question. So-called misperception, atmospherics and electrical storms were all the order of the day, although certainly not everyone agreed with that assertion.

Via a contact that he enigmatically describes as having a 'close association' with GCHQ, Robin Cole learned that during the early hours of the morning of 5 October 1996, two senior civil servants were ordered to report to GCHQ to carry out 'a full analysis of the situation'.

'I know their occupations and I even have their names now,' states Mr. Cole. 'But, the problem is, if I give out too much information, I'll identify them. At this stage I don't want to do that, but I can tell you that one was an extremely high-up civil servant who looks at different situations which the Government finds itself in almost the point of view of a sociologist, saying: "How are the general public going to perceive this position that we find ourselves in?" and things like that.

But as Robin Cole delved further into the hidden world of GCHQ, he learned that their involvement in the UFO subject did not solely centre on the events of October 1996. He also discovered that GCHQ's library holds a number of books on the UFO subject. 'Again,' he states, 'I don't want to reveal too much about the source of this information, but they, too, have a close association to GCHQ. GCHQ has this very extensive library of books and manuscripts, and the employees are apparently allowed access to it. But I was most interested when somebody from GCHQ asked me if I had a copy of the U.S. Air Force's UFO investigation study, *Project Blue Book*. When I said no, they said that they had a copy at work. It turns out that GCHQ has 15 or 20 UFO books in its library.'

Mr. Cole elaborates further about GCHQ's role in the study of the UFO phenomena, saying:

> 'One GCHQ source lives literally across the road from a friend and colleague of mine. They got talking about UFOs one day, and this person said: "I know nothing compared to what other departments know. But, yes, occasionally we did track objects that defied all rational explanation, and I know that the speed and agility of the objects is just unbelievable."'

That same source also confided that those within GCHQ tasked with examining such data were convinced they were dealing with an alien technology infinitely more advanced than that of 20th century mankind.

Surely the most bizarre story to reach Mr. Cole, however, came from a woman whose job involved analysing Signals Intelligence data at GCHQ.

> 'The woman came home from work one afternoon and said to her brother: "Look, I've got something really serious to tell you, but you're not to tell anybody else. We've known for years that we're at war with these beings." She didn't really say much more than that, apart from the fact that the UFO issue was a very serious one.'

Despite the seemingly incredible nature of the data imparted to Mr. Cole, there is demonstrable evidence to show that his research hit a very raw nerve within the secret world of officialdom. Having obtained an extraordinary body of information linking GCHQ with UFOs, in 1997, Mr. Cole put all of his findings together into a self-published report. He takes up the story, saying:

> 'Just after my report was published, I was interviewed with regard to its contents by *Central TV*. Then, the following morning the phone rang and it was a Detective Sergeant by the name of Tim Camp from Cheltenham Special Branch. He made it clear that he wanted to interview me.'

Mr. Cole continued that shortly afterwards D.S. Camp arrived, and the questions took a curious turn. 'Who do you work for…what's your interest in the UFO phenomena…what do you do?' Eventually, D.S. Camp departed, apparently satisfied with the answers that Mr. Cole supplied.

However, the apparent official interest in his activities continued. On several occasions, Mr. Cole had seen an unusual looking van parked outside his second-storey flat – right next to the telephone junction-box…

This could, of course, have been entirely innocent – were it not for the fact that a trusted, insider contact was able to track the ownership of the vehicle (via its registration plate) to a Ministry of Defence post office box in Wiltshire! As a result of probing into the top secret links between UFOs and GCHQ, Mr. Cole has apparently attracted the attention of Special Branch and elements of the MoD.

To this day, Robin Cole is unsure what to make of the GCHQ-UFO connection, but of one thing he is certain: 'The British Government states that UFOs are of no defence significance. I would say in response that as far as UFOs are concerned, the government can offer us no significant defence.'

There can be very few British people who are not at least vaguely familiar with a certain Gary McKinnon. Yep, you've got it right: he's that poor sod who potentially faces decades in a U.S. prison for hacking into the classified files of Uncle Sam, in search of top-secret data on all-things flying and saucer-shaped, no less. But, years before Gary hit the 'UFO-hacking' scene, there was a certain Matthew Bevan; a good friend of Matthew Williams and someone who I got to know quite well in the late-1990s. Just like Gazza, Bevvers was into computers, hacking and UFOs. And it all got him into very big trouble with the boys from Scotland Yard – as my article for *The Planet on Sunday* on the man himself, titled *The Riddle of Hangar 18*, demonstrated:

O f the many rumours and allegations that surround the on-going UFO controversy, one absolutely refuses to die: namely, that at Wright-Patterson Air Force base in Dayton, Ohio, USA, there exist a series of secret rooms, aircraft hangars and underground chambers. This is where the preserved remains of a number of dead alien creatures are, it is claimed, stored; along with the wreckage of their crashed and recovered UFO.

Further rumours assert that the alien technology has now been secretly duplicated and the U.S. military is busy at work building and flying its own prototype UFOs. In generic terms, the location of this astonishing other-worldly evidence has become known as *Hangar 18*. Officially, the U.S. Government denies that such stories have any basis in fact whatsoever, but an impressive body of testimony from a number of high-ranking and on-the-record sources suggests otherwise.

The late US senator, Barry Goldwater, for example, stated in 1975 that: 'The subject of UFOs is one that has interested me for some long time. About ten or twelve years ago I made an effort to find out what was in the building at Wright-Patterson Air Force Base where the information is stored that has been collected by the Air Force, and I was understandably denied this request. It is still classified above Top Secret.'

A similar account comes from no less a source than a former executive assistant to the deputy director, and special assistant to the executive director, of the Central Intelligence Agency, one Victor Marchetti. Revealing that during his time with the CIA, UFOs came under the category of 'very sensitive activities', Mr. Marchetti states that he personally heard from 'high levels' within the CIA that the bodies of 'little grey men', whose UFO had crashed, were stored at the Foreign Technology Division of Wright-Patterson Air Force Base.

While such information has been scoffed at by the sceptics, it has now received a major boost from a wholly unexpected source: namely, a brilliant young computer hacker operating from the comfort of his Cardiff home.

As an experienced hacker of literally thousands of computer systems, including those of NASA and the United States' Defence Department, Matthew Bevan took the decision back in 1994 to uncover the UFO secrets of Wright-Patterson Air Force Base.

Stressing that Wright-Patterson was 'a very, very easy computer system to get into', he was amazed to uncover astonishing information relating to an ultra-secret project to design and build a truly extraordinary flying machine.

'The files,' he states today, 'very clearly referred to a working prototype of an anti-gravity vehicle that utilised a heavy element to power it. This wasn't a normal aircraft; it was very small, split level, with a reactor at the bottom and room for the crew at the top.'

Having accessed and digested the information, Mr. Bevan duly exited the Wright-Patterson computer banks and began to search elsewhere. He had got in, carefully read the files, and made good his escape, all without any form of detection.

Or: so he thought...

For two years there was silence. Then, on a morning in 1996, everything suddenly changed. At the time, Mr. Bevan was working for an insurance company in Cardiff and on the day in question was summoned down to the Managing Director's office. On entering the room, he was confronted by a group of men, and Mr. Bevan recalls what happened next.

'One of the men outstretched his hand and I shook it. "Matthew Bevan?" he asked.

"Yes," I replied. He said: "My name is Detective Sergeant Simon Janes of Scotland Yard's Computer Crimes Unit, and I'm placing you under arrest for hacking NASA and Wright-Patterson Air Force Base."'

On being taken to Cardiff Central Police Station, the line of questioning became decidedly curious: 'What does the term *Hangar 18* mean to you?' Bevan was asked.

'That's a hoarding place for alien technology,' he replied, nonchalantly.

Today, Bevan's recollections of that exchange are more than eye-opening. 'Throughout the interview, they kept coming back to *Hangar 18*: Did I see anything on the Wright-Patterson computers? Did I download anything? Well, when they asked me if I saw anything, I said: "Yes, an anti-gravity propulsion system."'

Needless to say, this did not go down too well. Mr. Bevan was in big trouble and a date was set for a hearing at London's Bow Street magistrate's court. But: it was not just Mr. Bevan, his defence, and the prosecution who were present. A certain Jim Hanson, representing the interests of the U.S. Government, was also in attendance.

There was a curious exchange when Hanson took the stand – as Mr. Bevan remembers only too well. 'As the hearing continued, the prosecution asked Hanson what the American Government thought about my motives regarding my hacking at Wright-Patterson,' said Mr. Bevan.

'Hanson replied: "We now believe that Mr. Bevan had no malicious intentions and that his primary purpose was to uncover information on UFOs and *Hangar 18*."

Mr. Bevan says: 'Well, *everyone* had a bit of a laugh at that point; however, when the prosecution asked: "Can you confirm if *Hangar 18* exists or if it's a myth?" Hanson said:

"I can neither confirm nor deny as I'm not in possession of that information."'

The final outcome: the case against Mr. Bevan collapsed. The magistrate overseeing the case stated in no uncertain terms that a jail sentence was out of the question, and any fine that he could impose would be meagre.

Coupled with the fact that the Americans were unwilling to divulge information concerning the contents of the Wright-Patterson computers to the court, and the cost of prosecuting the case was perceived as being as high as $10,000 a day, the prosecution offered no evidence.

Mr. Bevan was a free man.

Hangar 18 might not have revealed all of its secrets for the world to see, and yet there is no doubt that from his Cardiff home, Mr. Bevan came very close to uncovering the full truth that lies behind Wright-Patterson Air Force Base's involvement in the UFO controversy – a truth apparently guarded with an almost paranoid zeal by the U.S. Government for decades.

Mr. Bevan states that his computer hacking days are now well and truly behind him, but it seems inevitable that one day yet another Matthew Bevan will come along to test Wright-Patterson's house of UFO secrets. *Hangar 18* will almost certainly one day be opening its doors for all to see. Of course, whether or not this will be with the full knowledge and consent of the U.S. Government is an entirely different matter.

***

And then there was the very intriguing story of a certain Bill Maguire that I splashed across the pages of *The Planet on Sunday*:

Eye-Witness Encounters

In 1952, William Maguire was stationed at RAF Sennen, near Land's End in Cornwall, where he worked as a radar specialist. As a regular in the RAF, his skills were in high demand and his position as a senior aircraftsman meant that he and a team of five others often worked together at different bases in order to give accurate readings of radar instruments.

> 'These were usually during exercises and there would usually be the same half a dozen of us. Usually, it was made clear to us where we were going. You'd get a travel warrant and a truck would be waiting to pick you up.'

On one occasion, Maguire and his colleagues were driven to a location which he now believes to be somewhere near RAF Sandwich in Kent. From the onset Maguire realised that this exercise was going to be different to all the previous ones, because the windows of the truck, which on previous occasions had been open, were all shuttered. When the team got to the location they found it was an open field with a hump which led to a large underground installation.

'Even in those days, this place impressed me,' he says.

'This was a huge complex; I'd never seen the likes of it before. It must have gone down for half a mile. It was like something out of a science-fiction film: everywhere was lit up in blue light and it was completely operational with about 100 people working there.'

As Maguire explains, the machinery in this underground labyrinth superseded any that was being used at that point for the purpose of detection and observation.

> 'As an experienced radar operator, what surprised me most was the extent of the machines. They were able to see right across to Eastern Europe and parts of Russia and way over to Sweden, which I hadn't realised at that time we could do.
>
> 'My memory was that everything was in a complete flap. Normally, in a military situation everything is ordered, regular and set out. But here was a situation that was plainly out of control. Mechanics were flying about all over the place.'

As Maguire got his bearings and the situation was revealed to him in its starkest form, the reasons behind the blind panic became staggeringly clear – a huge, unidentified aerial object was being tracked on the radar-scopes high over the English Channel.

> 'The mechanics were being blamed for not calibrating the instruments

properly; we were being blamed for not interpreting the readings correctly. Every single instrument on the base was showing this enormous object sitting up at an unbelievable height. It was the size of a warship and it just stood there.'

At the time, Maguire and his colleagues did not interpret this as an alien spaceship. 'There was talk of an escaped V-2 rocket – which was rubbish – and temperature inversions. But we knew damned well what an inversion was. We could tell an inverted seagull, never mind something as big as a warship.'

Maguire recalls that the object stayed in the same position for 18 minutes before splitting into three parts and disappearing at phenomenal speed. One went north, one south towards France, and the third, east to the Balkans.

> 'Whatever this thing was, it had sat stationary in a stratospheric wind of several hundred miles per hour – which was quite colossal for the time. I wasn't on the height finder but I remember the mechanics said that it was higher than anything we knew about.'

Afterwards, Maguire and his colleagues were told by their seniors not to talk about the incident. 'It was all brushed under the carpet and we were all split up. But I do remember coming out at night and looking up and thinking: I wonder what the hell that was?'

Whatever it was that William Maguire and a whole team of experienced radar personnel tracked from that vast underground complex nearly fifty years ago, it is still something of a mystery Even so, Maguire is no longer afraid to talk about the event. 'I'm seventy years old. What are they going to do? I don't feel tied by the secrecy act. All I know is that something was up there.'

Foot & Mouth Conspiracy or Accident? 2001

Very few British people, I'm sure, will ever forget the stark and ominous sight of cattle-upon-cattle piled high and burning at the height of the nation's foot-and-mouth outbreak of 2001, and which provoked Armageddon-like imagery just about here, there and everywhere across the land. In a very weird twist of fate, when the outbreak was at its absolute fiercest, I was in the United States: spending a week or thereabouts at the National Archives, Maryland with MJ12 researcher/author Ryan Wood. Digging through a near-foot-high stack of old and faded files late one afternoon, I was startled to the core to come across a sizeable collection of material that demonstrated how – back in the late 1940s and into the early 1950s - the U.S. Government had secretly expressed deep concerns that terrorists might very well try and cripple the U.S. cattle-herd via a deliberate unleashing of nothing less than foot-and-mouth disease. Of course, given what was afoot back in Britain at the very same time that I was reading this extraordinary material, this got my conspiratorial mind in a veritable whirl: could it possibly have been the case that there was far more than meets the eye to the foot-and-mouth scare of a decade ago? To this day, I still have to wonder; as I did in late-2001, when I prepared the following article – titled *Foot & Mouth: Conspiracy or Accident?* – for Mark Birdsall's *Eye-Spy Magazine* (and which, in an abbreviated format, also appeared in the *Walsall Express & Star* and the *Western Daily Press* newspapers):

In an intriguing and decidedly unexpected twist on the foot-and-mouth disease crisis which affected much of Britain's cattle herd in 2000 (and in a fashion that is sure to intrigue both conspiracy theorists and those tasked with officially assessing the threat posed to the world by biological warfare today), formerly Top Secret papers have surfaced under the terms of the United States Government's Freedom of Information Act showing that more than 50 years ago, American authorities were concerned that a potentially-hostile nation would attempt to destroy the US food chain by deliberately infecting the country's cattle herd with foot-and-mouth and other potentially crippling diseases.

Prepared under cover of the strictest security by the Committee on Biological Warfare and at the request of the American Government's elite Research and Development Board, the fifty-page file in question dates from March 1947 through to the latter part of 1948 and makes for highly disturbing reading. Not only that: it also demonstrates that within the corridors of power there were dark fears concerning the future of international warfare.

In a Top Secret paper of 28 March 1947 it was stated that:

> "A memorandum from the Secretaries of War and Navy dated 21 February 1947, Subject: *International Aspects of Biological Warfare*, regarding biological warfare in relation to United Nations negotiations for regulation of armaments was referred by the Board to Committee 'X' for consideration and recommendations."

Seven months later, the Research and Development Board prepared an in-depth report (that was also classified Top Secret) that outlined its deep concerns with respect to biological warfare operations and the potential threat posed to the United States of America.

As the Board stated:

> "Preparations for biological warfare can be hidden under a variety of guises. The agents of biological warfare are being studied in every country of the world because they are also the agents of diseases of man, domestic animals and crop plants. The techniques used in developing biological warfare agents are essentially similar to the techniques used in routine bacteriological studies and in the production of vaccines, toxoids and other beneficial materials."

In its report, the Board continued:

> "...the Committee feels that although it may be possible to control atomic research and insure that it be devoted to peaceful purposes, it is impracticable to control research on biological agents because of the close similarity between such research and legitimate investigations of a medical, agricultural or veterinary nature."

But what of the possibility that biological warfare could have been utilized as a weapon of mass destruction and the cause of extreme devastation? In 1947, as we shall now see, the Board had its doubts that biological warfare could be considered to be a tool of destruction on a par with atomic weapons; however, as we will soon learn, only twelve months later that view had changed radically within the higher echelons of the Research and Development Board.

With respect to this matter, in October 1947, the Board wrote that:

> " On the basis of present knowledge the Committee feels that biological weapons cannot be compared in their effect with such so-called weapons of mass destruction as, for example, the atomic bomb. It is doubtless true that if a self-sustaining epidemic of a fatal disease could be established in a human population, indiscriminate destruction of life on a great scale might result. However, as has been pointed out earlier in this discussion, the Committee knows of no epidemic agent that could presently be used with confidence in its significant epidemic-producing property. The spread of epidemics depends upon a number of complex inter-related factors, many of which are poorly understood or perhaps even unknown. Furthermore, it is believed that the chances of discovering an unusually virulent epidemic-producing biological agent is highly improbable and cannot be anticipated at any time in the predictable future."

So much for the Committee's beliefs with respect to biological warfare and the Human Race; however, on the issue of the animal kingdom, it stated that:

> "The statements made in the preceding paragraph do not apply equally well to epizootic agents. Within this group are highly infectious agents that the Committee believes could be used to cause widespread epizootics in domestic animal populations. However, these agents could not be considered as a means of indiscriminate destruction of life in terms of human beings."

The Committee continued in its 1947 report:

> "As far as non-epidemic producing agents are concerned, the Committee feels that the use of these as weapons would cause no more indiscriminate destruction of life than would, for example, use of incendiary munitions. Also destruction of property would be practically nil with biological agents, whereas it is considerable with conventional incendiary or explosive munitions. While it is granted that innocent civilians would be affected by all biological agents, the same can be said for any type of explosive munitions. Furthermore, since non-epidemic agents do not spread rapidly from one individual to another, an attack with these agents would be as indiscriminate and probably as localised as would an attack with incendiary bombs or high explosive munitions."

In conclusion, it was stated that:

> "As a matter of fact, predictions of effectiveness of biological agents against a human population must be taken with reservations. No experimental animal is available that can be used to measure the effectiveness of these weapons against man. For these reasons the Committee feels that at present biological warfare cannot be correctly classed as a means of mass destruction of human beings. The use of most biological agents might be more humane and less objectionable than the use of conventional weapons, for two reasons. In the first place, property is not destroyed in biological warfare and production facilities of a defeated nation may recover more quickly than if large amounts of property were destroyed. In the second place, destruction of life may be less with biological warfare if debilitating but non-fatal agents are used. For example, the use of the agent causing undulant fever as an offensive weapon might be expected to cause large numbers of casualties and thus greatly aid the war effort of the attacking nation, but most of the casualties would recover after a period of illness and could resume active lives."

With that, the Committee chairman, Vannevar Bush, prepared a confidential memorandum for the Joint Chiefs of Staff that summarised the Committee's findings and recommendations with respect to biological warfare from a defensive perspective.

However, by the latter part of 1948, as will now become starkly apparent, biological warfare was seen as a major threat to the USA by the Research and Development Board. Moreover, the terrifying fear that a hostile nation would attempt to ravage the US food-supply by deliberately infecting its cattle herd with rampant diseases was running high in official circles.

According to the 1948 documents at issue:

> "Biological warfare lends itself especially well to undercover operations, particularly because of the difficulty in detecting such operations and because of the versatility possible by the proper selection of biological warfare agents."

The Committee continued:

> "Within the last few years there have been several outbreaks of exotic diseases and insect pests which are believed to have been introduced accidentally but which could have been introduced intentionally had someone wished to do so. The use of epizootic agents against our animal population by sabotage methods is a very real and immediate danger. Foot-and-mouth disease and rinderpest are among those which would spread rapidly, and unless effective counter-measures were immediately applied, would seriously affect the food supply of animal origin."

Much grimmer still is the following extract:

> "Since foot-and-mouth is now present in Mexico, it would be relatively easy for saboteurs to introduce the disease into the United States and have this introduction appear as natural spread from Mexico. Since rinderpest and foot-and-mouth disease are not present in the United States, our animal population is extremely vulnerable to these diseases."

Alarmingly, the papers reveal, the United States was (and logic dictates, still is) in no position to prevent a large-scale biological assault on its animal population had it indeed occurred:

> "The United States is particularly vulnerable to this type of attack. It is believed generally that espionage agents of foreign countries which are potential enemies of the United States are present already in this country. There appears to be no great barrier to prevent additional espionage agents from becoming established here and there is no control over the movements of people within the United States."

The document continues:

> "North America is an isolated land mass and hence specific areas therein present feasible biological warfare targets for an extra-continental enemy since fear of backfiring is minimised."

Most disturbing, however, was the potential outlook for the USA in the event of a country-wide biological warfare attack on the country's cattle herd utilising devastating diseases as a tool of biological warfare:

> "The food supply of the nation could be depleted to an extent which materially would reduce the nation's capacity to defend itself and to wage war. Serious outbreaks of disease of man, animals or plants also would result in profound psychological disturbances."

But how would a covert introduction of such diseases into the US food chain be undertaken? The Committee had a number of ideas: via "water contamination"; "fodder and food"; "infected bait"; "contamination of soil"; "Biological Warfare aerosols"; and deliberate "contamination of veterinary pharmaceuticals and equipment."

The results envisaged back in 1948 parallel precisely and eerily the scenario that was seen in the United Kingdom during its foot-and-mouth crisis of 2000: "a reduction of meat supply"; "disruption of economic balance"; "reduction of animal transport"; and most illuminating of all: "Establishment of a source of infection for man."

Realizing the potentially grave implications that such a scenario presented, the United States' Government carefully and quietly began to initiate a number of plans to try and combat any possible attack on the continental United States that might have occurred. Recommending that a special unit should be established to deal with the situation, the Committee asserted that ventilation shafts, subway systems and water supplies throughout the country should be carefully monitored. Similarly, the Committee stated, steps should be taken to determine:

> "the extent to which contamination of stamps, envelopes, money, cosmetics, food and beverages as a means of subversively disseminating biological agents is possible."

In addition to preparing for the worst from a defensive perspective, however, United States authorities were not above planning their own biological warfare operations from an offensive perspective.

> "Major goals and objectives of a research and development programme in the field of offensive special biological warfare operations include:
>
> (1) Development of new agents suitable for special operations;
> (2) development of methods of dissemination for special BW operations;
> (3) determination of effectiveness and feasibility of methods of dissemination; and
> (4) estimation of approximate dosages required for specific special BW operations."

But it was in the conclusions of the Committee's report on the deliberate use of animal-based diseases and other diseases as biological weapons that the utter lack of defence against such an attack was spelled out.

> "It is concluded that:
>
> (1) biological agents would appear to be well adapted to subversive use.
> (2) The United States is particularly susceptible to attack by special BW operations.
> (3) The subversive use of biological agents by a potential enemy prior to a declaration of war presents a grave danger to the United States.
> (4) The biological warfare research and development programme is not now authorised to meet the requirements necessary to prepare defensive measures against special BW operations."

Indeed, such was the concern shown that even the Federal Bureau of Investigation got in on the act. A confidential memorandum to FBI Director, J. Edgar Hoover on 9 May 1950 from

Raymond P. Whearty, Chairman, Interdepartmental Committee on Internal Security and titled *Alerting of Public Health Agencies re Biological Warfare*, states:

> "The Public Health Services has a long-established relationship (direct or through regional offices) with official State—and through them to local—health agencies. Accordingly, the Public Health Service should be the chief agency on which NSRB ** will rely as a source of advice to these agencies on biological warfare matters in so far as they are a part of civil defence of people. NSRB will rely on the Bureau of Animal Industry in the same manner for defence of animals against BW. The National Security Resources Board has kept the Public Health Service fully informed as to biological warfare plans. In developing these plans the NSRB created an Interdepartmental Committee on Defence Against Biological Warfare. The Public Health Service and BAI are, of course, represented on this committee. Definite plans are being made in this field, as shown by the two attached "Restricted" documents. The Public Health Services and Bureau of Animal Industry are planning the training course for civil defence against biological warfare and will conduct such courses if and when appropriations are available. Approximately fifty Public Health Service top administrative officers recently spent one week at Camp Detrick for orientation in BW as part of the training, for Public Health Service officers in this particular field."

As this document makes abundantly clear, numerous United States Government agencies in the late 1940s and early 1950s were implicated in the biological warfare issue as it specifically related to animals and the Bureau of Animal Industry. But that is not all.

Also contained within the released files are various "Withdrawal Notices" where certain documents have been withheld from public consumption and scrutiny on the grounds of national security. More than half a century on, it seems, some of the US Government's findings on biological warfare as they relate to animals - and particularly cattle - remain classified. Nevertheless, there is further evidence to support the notion that some outbreaks of animal-based diseases within the confines of the US in the 1940s and 1950s were not as innocent as might have been imagined at first glance.

In March 1957, former FBI Special Agent Guy Banister (who, curiously, would later become deeply implicated in the assassination of United States' President John F. Kennedy in November 1963) testified before the Louisiana Joint Legislative Committee and stated while working in the Pacific Northwest:

> "I recall one outbreak of hoof and mouth disease which occurred in dairy herds in Canada. Legally, it was not possible to establish that it was done – planted there. But an intelligence officer is never quite satisfied with a legal definition. And I have talked to many men. You can't be certain. We can't be

---

** Author's Note: The National Security Resources Board

certain that the man who was supposed to have taken it there was the one who actually did. Someone else could have put it there. We have the example of the 'wheat stem rust,' which hit Durham wheat where we get our macaroni. That was an up-flare. In that case I talked to the nation's leading plant pathologists in that field. We don't know where those spores came from. They trapped them at 15,000 feet in the air. Maybe it's a test run. We don't know. Maybe it's natural. But we must be suspicious now. We can't afford to pass it off as natural."

We would be wise to be aware that there are far more effective – and far stranger – tools of warfare than the bullet and the bomb. We might also want to consider the possibility that Britain's very own outbreak of foot-and-mouth disease in 2000 was not quite as innocent as might have been imagined...until now…

The C-Files - 2000/2001:

Just before *X-Files* mania finally imploded upon itself, Mike Lockley, the editor of the *Chase Post* newspaper, invited me and Irene Bott, the 'Staffordshire Dominatrix' herself (as Andy Roberts preferred to term the former head-honcho of the *Staffordshire UFO Group*!), to pen a regular, weekly column for the newspaper; which covered (and, to this day, continues to cover) the Staffordshire town of Cannock and its immediate surroundings. The column was, somewhat predictably and inevitably, titled *The C-Files*, and saw me playing Fox Mulder to Irene's Dana Scully. I think we wrote somewhere in the region of 15 or 16 items between mid-2000 and the time I fled Blighty for pastures new, in the Land of the Free (or, it was until Cheney and the Patriot Act surfaced from the pits of hell and left their vile marks on the nation's landscape and culture), in late 2001. And, here's a small and varied selection of those very same items. The first one led a sizeable number of people to come forward, and whose testimony was included in my 2007 book, *Man-Monkey: In Search of the British Bigfoot*.

Man-Monkeys and Big Cats:
Since the publication of our last *C-Files* feature, a number of important developments have occurred. Firstly, there has been another sighting of the Chase's very own big cat – this time by a man who had been driving through Chase Terrace on his way to Hammerwich at 5am on the morning of August 3. He skidded his van to a halt when he saw, on a car-park near the *Wych Elm* pub, a huge cat-like creature leisurely strolling along! He told us that it was as big as a Rottweiler dog, brown in colour, with a white tip on its tale. We'll keep you posted in further developments.

But that is not all. We have also been looking at a number of historical mysteries involving unknown animals that have occurred in the vicinity of the Chase, and have uncovered details of what is surely one of the most macabre stories of all: the Man-Monkey of Ranton...
It was the night of January 1, 1879, and a man was riding home from Woodcote to Ranton, Staffordshire. All was normal until around 10pm, when approximately a mile from the village of Woodseaves, and while crossing a bridge, he got the shock of his life: out of the trees leapt a horrific-looking creature. Jet-black in colour and with a pair of huge, glowing eyes, it was described by the petrified witness as being half-man and half-monkey!

Naturally, all hell broke loose. The creature jumped onto the back of the man's horse – which proceeded to bolt out of sheer fright – and a fierce battle began. Incredibly, according to the witness, when he attempted to hit the beast with his whip, it simply passed straight through its body! Suddenly, and without warning, the spectral 'manimal' vanished into thin-air, leaving one exhausted horse and its shell-shocked owner in a state of near-collapse.

Rushing to a nearby inn at Woodseaves for a much-needed drink, the man recounted his story to a concerned crowd. He then headed off home and retired to bed – where he apparently spent several days in a state of exhaustion.

But that is not the end of the tale. Several days later, a somewhat exaggerated account reached the ears of the local constabulary. A policeman was dispatched to the home of the man's employer to ascertain the truth. Had some form of crime occurred? Who was the mystery assailant? The police wanted answers. However, when the man's employer relayed the facts, it was the policeman who had a comment to make: 'Oh, is that all, sir? I know what that was. That was the Man-Monkey, sir, as does come again at that bridge ever since the man was drowned in the cut.'

So what was the mysterious creature? The folklorist Charlotte S. Burne published details in 1883 (after having spoken directly with the employer of the witness). However, since then the story has remained tantalisingly unresolved and no-one seems to know how on earth the unnamed policeman came to be so well informed about the identity of the creature.

We asked Richard Freeman, who between 1986 and 1990 was a head keeper at Twycross Zoo and who now devotes his life to investigating and writing about mysterious animals, such as Bigfoot, the Loch Ness Monster and, of course, the big-cats of the Chase, for an opinion.

Richard told us that he has come across a number of similar reports from both Scotland and the wilds of Exmoor and is convinced that these are supernatural creatures (as opposed to flesh-and-blood animals) that may be responsible for the ancient legends of trolls (which, like the Man-Monkey of Ranton, were supposed to live under or near bridges) that were so prevalent in years gone-by. A supernatural entity or: simply an escaped monkey? This *C-File*, it seems, is destined to remain unexplained.

We also related to Richard the details of our most recent *C-File* on the Cannock Chase big-cat

The Lair of the Man-Monkey.

and he was certain in his view that: 'What you have just described is a puma; no doubt about it.' The beasts of the Chase, it seems, are not going to go away.

The Old Sink with Hot and Cold Running Ghouls:
With Halloween only around the corner, we thought this month we would try and come up with something suitably spooky for you. As it turns out, this has not proven to be a difficult task at all!

Just recently we have investigated haunting, poltergeists and spectral figures seen in the vicinity of the Chase. However, what is surely the strangest case to catch our attention concerns a series of eerie-looking images of faces that have appeared on, of all things, an old kitchen sink!

The husband and wife who own the sink have asked not to be identified – and will hereafter be referred to as Mr. and Mrs. X – but have allowed us to relate their remarkable account for readers of *The C-Files*. And what an account it is!

The couple live in a mid-1940s property that backs on to the Chase and the sink was one of the original fittings. However, in later years it was taken out and stored away in their garage – until 1996, that is, when the couple decided to convert it into a garden accessory complete with plants and gnomes.

On August 1 of this year, however, something very strange occurred. On opening the curtains of their living-room, Mrs. X was shocked to see what seemed to be a face staring back at her from the side of the old sink. She quickly called her husband, who also saw the remarkable spectacle – as did their sons. But what – or rather who – was it? Mrs. X told us that several people said at the time the face looked like the popular image people have of Jesus.

Others, however, thought the face resembled someone from the era of the Cavaliers. Then something weirder took place: other faces began to appear on the side of the sink, including those of an old man and what seemed to be the face of a lion. Interestingly, Mrs. X told us that a local vicar visited their property and a suggestion was made one of the faces looked like the image on the 'Turin Shroud'.

It may not be entirely coincidental, therefore, that the appearance of the first face happened only five days before what is known as 'Transfiguration Day' – the date on which people all around the world claim to see faces with a religious connection on stonework, in churches and elsewhere.

But: what of the suggestion that the face was not unlike someone from the era of the Cavaliers? Oddly enough, the area in which Mr. and Mrs. X live is near the site of a historic conflict: the Battle of Hopton Heath. Moreover, a search of the back garden of their property with a metal-detector uncovered various items such as coins and lead-shot dating back to the time of the Cavaliers.

When we first learned the details of this fascinating account, we naturally asked if we could take a look at the evidence ourselves. Mrs. X was happy to oblige – and, sure enough, the images are there and they do appear to show human faces and are incredibly realistic.
 Do the faces have a religious link? Or is it possible there may be a connection with the Battle of Hopton Heath and the spirit of a long dead Cavalier? Mrs. X stated: 'I'd love to know why this has happened to us.' And so would we. Doubtless, we have not heard the end of this story. Should the truth, indeed, be out there, we'll let you know.

Tale of a Chase Hi-Tech Triangle:
You may recall that a number of weeks ago we devoted our *C-Files* feature to a discussion of a series of sightings of UFOs in the Cannock Chase area that had been dubbed the 'Flying Triangles'. Typically, these were described as being large, black-coloured machines that were seen flying around the Chase in the dead of night and in almost complete silence. As we also revealed, reports of encounters with the Chase's Flying Triangles had even reached the eyes and ears of the Ministry of Defence at Whitehall!

When the feature was published, we expected to receive some feedback; however, even we were unprepared for the absolute deluge of reports that poured in. From across the entire area and covering the last 20 years, it seems, the Flying Triangles have been out in force. Of the many accounts that were brought to our attention, however, one stood out more than any other.

It was at approximately 8.30pm on an autumn evening in 1985 that a father and son were driving across the Cannock Chase towards Rugeley, having been to Penkridge to purchase a motorbike. They passed the *White House* pub and all was normal – that is, until they rounded the bend near the rifle-range. As they did so, both father and son were shocked and amazed to see sitting in the sky at a distance of 100 feet and at a height of no more than 150 feet, a large, black, triangular-shaped object that was lit up by three lights attached to its underside.

They screeched the car to a halt, jumped out and stared in awe at the incredible spectacle. For a moment the object simply hung there in utter silence above the silhouetted trees of the forest; but then without warning it shot away at an incredible speed. Both father and son looked at each other and then raced for the car and headed home to Rugeley.

On arriving, the father telephoned the local police to report what had occurred. Interestingly, the police responded immediately and two uniformed officers arrived on their doorstep post-haste. Detailed witness statements were taken from the two men who, significantly, were informed by the officers: 'You know, you should never have got out of the car.' Precisely why this piece of advice was given was never made clear; however, the police did admit that a report on their encounter had been forwarded to the Ministry of Defence.

To this day, the father and son told us, no explanation has been forthcoming as to why the police responded with such unusual speed to their UFO sighting on the Cannock Chase. Is it possible that officers out on patrol had also seen the mysterious object and that this had a bear ing on the seriousness with which the encounter was treated? If that is the case and you were one of the officers, give us a call. Someone, or something, with the benefit of an incredibly advanced technology is using the Chase for...well, who knows what? It's about time we found out. And if we do, let's hope that it's good news...

Satellites from the Skies: 2001

In the first week of 2001, I wrote an article for the *Daily Express* titled: *Just What Would Happen if a Satellite Fell from the Sky?* The subject of the two-page feature was a leaked Home Office file on how the British Government might secretly handle the crash of a hazardous, nuclear-powered satellite on jolly old Britain. A decade on, I can now reveal that the file in question had been leaked to none other than crop-circle constructer and Rudloe Manor penetrator Matthew Williams, by a certain source with deep, official connections. The conspiracy-theorists are, no doubt, now having a veritable field day, as a result of that intriguing revelation! Here's the article, in full:

There can be few unaware of the frenzy that accompanied news from Russia that, at Christmas, contact was lost with its *Mir* space-station for a terrifying 20 hours. As the 140-tonne station hurtled around Earth, speculation was rife that *Mir* would spiral out of control and a disaster was imminent like that depicted in the film *Deep Impact*, shown on BBC1 last night, in which a meteor hits our planet.

A calamity was averted when, as mission-control chief, Vladimir Sololyov, revealed on Boxing Day, contact with, and control of, *Mir* had been re-established. '*Mir* will not fall on your heads on New Year's Eve,' he said. 'We have a plan to bid farewell to *Mir* in a civilised and organised way.' He said *Mir* would be brought down in a controlled descent in the Pacific between February 27 and 28.

Throughout one of the tensest moments in the history of Russia's space-programme, officialdom was quick to state that the possibility of *Mir* crashing to Earth and wreaking untold havoc was remote. Perhaps. The *Daily Express*, however, has learned that the British Government has been acutely aware of the threat posed by satellites and space-stations in Earth's orbit, and has since at least 1979 had secret guidelines in place should the unthinkable occur. Via an insider source with the Home Office, we have been given access to a classified eight-page document that details how the Government, the military and the emergency services would respond if a satellite crashed on Britain.

Classified at *Restricted* level, and later upgraded to a higher level of security, the document, titled *Satellite Accidents with Radiation Hazards*, was prepared in 1979 by the Home Office and was circulated to every Chief Officer of Police, every Chief Fire Officer and every County Council in England and Wales. 'Similar circulars are being issued by the Scottish Office and the Northern Ireland Office,' said the author of the paper.

An examination of the file makes it clear that the Home Office's decision to circulate the document on such a large scale was, ostensibly at least, because of an event that had occurred twelve months previously – as the following extract from the file reveals:

> 'Following the descent of a nuclear-powered satellite in Canada on 24 January 1978, consideration has been given to contingency arrangements for dealing with the possibility of a similar incident in the United Kingdom.'

The Home Office added that the possibility of a nuclear-powered satellite crashing within the British Isles was 'remote.' However, it was careful to add that

> "the special considerations that affect the use of nuclear materials and the safety standards applied to them make it prudent to devise plans to deal with such an incident."

According to the file, one of the hardest predictions to make was when and where a stricken space vehicle, possibly spiralling wildly out of control and at hundreds, or even thousands, of miles-per-hour would impact. On this issue, the author of the document stated:

> 'Although it is likely that knowledge of changes in the orbital pattern which might lead to premature return to Earth would be available many hours or even days before re-entry occurred, it would not be such that a reasonably accurate prediction of the final orbit over the Earth could be made until 12 to 24 hours before impact. Even then forecasts of the precise point of re-entry along this track might still be in error by thousands of kilometres. It is possible accurate warning would not be available till a few minutes before impact and it is possible there might be no warning.'

The document also makes it very clear that the Home Office was well acquainted with the more technical aspects of satellite technology:

> 'Some satellites are designed in such a way that they will disintegrate on re-entry; others are so designed that fairly large components will remain intact on entering Earth's atmosphere.'

And, if a space vehicle were to impact on the British Isles, what would be the outcome? The author of the document had a few ideas:

> 'Although the parameters of the orbit of a crashing satellite can be fairly closely defined, debris might fall over an area 2,000 kilometres wide. It would not be possible to alert police forces on a selective basis. In the event of a warning that a satellite might crash in or near the UK, all police forces would be alerted.'

In other words, official authorities all across the nation would potentially be put on stand-by to deal with the crash and recovery of exotic, space-based technologies. And that would only be the beginning, as the file demonstrates:

> 'The crash of a nuclear-powered satellite would present problems such as: There would be a possible radiation hazard; debris from the crashed satellite might be scattered over a very large area, perhaps the greater part of the country; and the individual pieces of debris might be very small, yet each might present a small radiation hazard.'

> Most significant of all, however, is a section of the document that refers not to *when*, but *if* the public should be informed of such a disaster: 'A Government decision would then be sought on whether the police should be alerted and whether a public statement should be made. If such actions were to be decided upon, overall responsibility for the measures to deal with an incident would be exercised from a central point in Whitehall, in a manner similar to procedures already established to handle a terrorist incident.'

And who, precisely, would play a role in such recoveries? The list is intriguing, to say the least, and focused primarily upon the Atomic Weapons Research Establishment (AWRE) at Aldermaston; the National Radiological Protection Board (NRPB); the Ministry of Defence; and representatives from NAIR: the National Arrangements for Incidents involving Radioactivity. The Home Office then turned its attention to what would happen in the event that a crash was fully confirmed:

> 'When reports of suspected or actual locations have been received, the police should take such steps as may be needed locally to prevent people entering areas which may be dangerous because of radioactive material. All persons should be told to keep well away from possible radioactive debris. Although highly unlikely, some large pieces of debris might have radiation fields of significance over distances the order of 100 meters and some limited evacuation might be necessary; widespread continuous contamination is, however, unlikely.'

In the wake of such a crash, the Home Office realised, the identification and collection of highly-hazardous debris would be a painstaking process:

> 'Since much of the debris would be very small, many of the fragments would not be sighted and unnoticed irradiated debris might well be scattered over thousands of square kilometres. A major search operation might have to be mounted to locate radioactive fragments. Whether to mount a search, and if so what area should be covered, would be decided by the central control point. Arrangements would be made to deploy the resources of every available technical support service, including teams from the Ministry of Defence, National Radiological Protection Board, United Kingdom Atomic Energy Authority, British Nuclear Fuels and Electricity Generating Boards, using specialist aircraft and vehicle search techniques. In rural areas, the most effective initial search to locate major sources of radioactivity might be from the air.'

Two further sections of the document stand out as being worthy of comment. The first, titled *Public Warning About Radioactivity*, provides further insight into the British Government's position on informing the populace at large of a disaster involving the crash of a contaminated spacecraft on British soil:

> 'It is for the Government to decide whether, and by what means, a public warning of danger from radioactivity should be given. In reaching that decision, the need to prevent unnecessary alarm would be carefully considered. Chief Officers should therefore ensure that nothing is done locally to anticipate a Government statement.'

So much for the public: but what of the media? Under the heading *Press and Publicity*, we learn the following:

> 'It is essential that those dealing with a satellite accident and the Government team in Whitehall should not issue inconsistent statements. Chief Officers should ensure that all local press enquiries are directed to a senior officer at force headquarters, who is briefed to deal with them, working in close liaison with Government information officers who would make appropriate arrangements to coordinate the national dissemination of information from Whitehall.'

In essence, that is the document. And although the leaked paper is now more than two decades old, there are several points worthy of comment. First, the Home Office was – and, logic dic tates, still is – very concerned by the possible scenario of a radioactive space vehicle crashing on British soil. Second, the fact that the public might be kept in the dark, if circumstances dictates, is highly worrying. One might ask: what gives the Government the right to decide whether members of the public are informed of the possibility that radioactive space debris might rain down on their heads? Should not such information be made public at the earliest opportunity?

A call to the Home Office's press room enticed a somewhat cagey response that affirmed the involvement of the Home Office in such matters today – along with the tracking-station at RAF Fylingdales, in Yorkshire. Official concern that one day a cosmic calamity will occur here of the sort that almost befell the *Mir* space station over Christmas, apparently, continues.

With the aforementioned document now squarely in the public domain, however, let us hope that we will see a change in procedures – a change that does not keep the average man, woman and child in ignorance of what may be going on in the skies above them.

Mystery on the Mountain 2001

Back in the late 1990s, I filed a Freedom of Information Act request with the CIA for documentation related to allegations that the agency had secretly found and recovered the remains of Noah's Ark. Yeah, I know: a very weird story indeed. But, it got even weirder when the CIA confirmed to me that they actually *did* have a file on Noah's Ark! My initial findings on the matter (that were updated in my 2004 book with Andy Roberts, titled *Strange Secrets*) appeared in the form of a two-page article for the *Western Daily Press* newspaper on July 3, 2001, under the headline of *Is This Really Noah's Ice Tomb?* This is it:

In a move certain to attract conspiracy theorists everywhere, the CIA has declassified 'an interim release of documents' concerning 'the possible remains of Noah's Ark on Mt. Ararat, Turkey'.

Rumours have long circulated that since the late 1940s, the CIA has been aware of, and has a bulky case file on, an impressive-looking, boat-like structure that sits within an icy tomb on the slopes of Mount Ararat – and that may well be the remains of Noah's mighty Ark.

So, the story goes, the 'Ararat Anomaly' (as the CIA describes it in typically bureaucratic style) was first noticed by U.S. military pilots undertaking a spying mission over the former Soviet Union in 1949. Since then, it has been alleged, numerous photographs and hours of film-footage of the Ark have been secured by the CIA, and by a host of other U.S. intelligence agencies, too.

Similarly, in a situation that mirrors the allegations of conspiracy and cover-up regarding the notorious 'Roswell Incident' of 1947, in which an alien craft and bodies were allegedly recovered by U.S. authorities, and the assassination of President John F. Kennedy in 1963, a whole host of claims, and counter-claims that would sit comfortably in an episode of *The X-Files* have surfaced regarding the Ark.

Shadowy sources tell of *Indiana Jones*-style expeditions to Turkey, secretly funded by the U.S. Government to try and locate the Ark. Others expand further and maintain that remnants of the Ark have been found and spirited away to classified military and governmental installations in America. And there is talk of intimidation by 'Men in Black'-type characters warning those with knowledge of the Ark to remain silent.

Far-fetched? Maybe. But not all of the claims can be discounted. Retired CIA operative Dino Brugioni, for example, has stated that the photographs, at least, most certainly do exist, and that a number that he viewed from the early 1970s did show what appeared to be 'three large curved wooded beams' on Mount Ararat.

But what of the CIA's newly-released file? Is it really a biblical smoking-gun? Or does it only confuse matters further, and add weight to the claims of cover-up and conspiracy? The answer may very well prove to be a combination of the two.

According to the Bible: 'God said unto Noah...Make thee an ark of gopher wood...And this is the fashion which thou shalt make it of: The length of the ark shall be three hundred cubits, the breadth of it fifty cubits, and the height of it thirty cubits.'

Moreover, it is alleged that the Ark was strong enough to withstand the catastrophic flood that allegedly encompassed the globe and lasted for forty turbulent days. So the story goes, when the flood waters began to recede, the Ark settled on its final resting place: the permanently snow-capped Mt. Ararat.

Needless to say, if the CIA has located the remains of such an impressive vessel, then it would undoubtedly be the scientific and archaeological discovery of the century. How would such a find by the CIA be made public? *Would* it be made public? And what does the agency's released file tell us?

Interestingly, the first entry in the file does not date from the immediate post-World War Two era. Nor has the CIA commented on the assertions of former CIA man Dino Brugioni. Rather, the first entry in the file dates from 1992 and is a letter from one Charles P. Aaron, described as being the 'Chief Pilot and Director of Operations' for the 'Tsirah Corporation'.

He wrote to the CIA requesting its assistance in the search for Noah's fabled vessel; a search that had been in progress for a number of years, and that had the support of the late astronaut Jim Irwin and several U.S. senators and congressmen.

Noteworthy is the fact that Aaron informed the CIA that several 'qualified officials' had informed him that the U.S. Government possessed a restricted-access satellite surveillance system that was capable of looking through ice. Aaron sensibly advised the CIA further that he was not interested in obtaining knowledge of what might have been classified surveillance-based technology; but simply wanted to know if the CIA could lend help to Tsirah's request to search the ice-covered peaks of Mount Ararat for the Ark. The CIA denied the request, and also denied any knowledge of such a satellite surveillance system. But the story of the CIA and the Ararat Anomaly is not quite over.

On January 21, 1993, the writer of a formerly secret CIA memorandum - that has since been declassified - made a curious reference to 'a request to declassify imagery of Noah's Ark for a TV production' that was, to quote further, 'turned down' by the CIA. It may be nothing more than a slip of the keyboard, but the specific reference to imagery of Noah's Ark (rather than, for example, imagery of the Ararat Anomaly, or imagery of an unidentified formation on Mt. Ararat) is something that we should bear in mind as potentially telling.

Of equal interest is a February 7, 1994, document from the CIA's Office of the Deputy Director for Science and Technology to the Director of Central Intelligence stating in part that they had: 'no efforts currently underway to conduct additional searches for Noah's Ark in the Mt. Ararat region'. Of course, the reference to 'additional searches' can only mean that at some point in its past, at least, the CIA *had* undertaken a quest to try and determine the truth about the Ararat Anomaly.

Whilst the allegations that imagery of the Ark exists in the vaults of the CIA cannot at this stage be conclusively confirmed, the existence of extensive CIA footage of the Mount Ararat region is not in dispute. Like the Roswell Incident and the JFK assassination, it is unlikely that the conspiracy theories surrounding Noah's Ark will fade and die anytime soon.

Cats on the Loose! (Page 101).

Something for the Weekend 2001

The Weekender was a newsstand magazine I wrote for in the early months of 2001. A glossy, full-colour, newsstand publication, *The Weekender* had an impressive circulation, and kept me in both pennies and *Carlsberg Special Brew* for a very welcome, albeit brief, period of time. From February to May, I penned three articles for the magazine. The first was titled *Uncovering the Real X-Files*, and went just like this:

As someone who works full-time as an author of books on the subject of unidentified flying objects, I am often asked why I am convinced that UFOs exist and why, in the words of *The X-Files*, the truth really is out there. Well, for me, it all began in 1978. At the time I hadn't really given UFOs any thought. However, it was in that year that my father related to me the details of a remarkable event that he'd been involved in back in September 1952.

At the time he was serving as a radar mechanic with the Royal Air Force at RAF Neatishead, Norfolk. He recalled that on several occasions strange things had occurred at the base: fast-moving, unidentified objects had been tracked on radar flying over the North Sea. Military aircraft had been scrambled to try and intercept the UFOs. The pilots reported that whatever the objects were, they were capable of travelling at fantastic speeds. But perhaps most significant of all was the fact that everyone involved was reminded sternly that they had signed the Official Secrets Act, and that they were not to discuss the incidents with anyone.

I never forgot what my father told me and it left a deep impression on me; to the extent that I decided one way or another, I would try and solve the mystery of what UFOs really were, once and for all.

Nearly a quarter of a century on since that fateful day in 1978, I can't say that I have all the answers. However, I can say that there is absolutely no doubt in my mind that UFOs do exist and that there are those within the British and American Governments who not only know this, but who will do their utmost to keep this information hidden from the general public.

I have met countless military personnel, radar operators, pilots and police officers who have seen UFOs and who have been ordered to remain silent by their superiors. I have interviewed a former United States Air Force Security Policeman who had a face-to-face encounter with a UFO in a Suffolk forest in December 1980.

I have travelled out to Nevada, home of the infamous Area 51, to speak with government employees engaged on super-secret UFO projects. And I have spoken with a British police officer who almost crashed his car into a UFO that was hovering at low-level over a road on the Yorkshire Moors in the early hours of a winter's morning many years ago.

But that is not all. The American and British Governments both operate a system that is designed to allow members of the public access to certain official files after a number of years. In Britain, this is known as the Thirty Year Ruling; and in the United States, it is referred to as the Freedom of Information Act. Via those acts, I have managed to secure from the CIA, FBI, National Security Agency, Ministry of Defence, Royal Air Force and countless others, thousands of pages of once-classified papers on UFOs.

Incredibly, the papers confirm that both military and airline pilots have seen UFOs. They confirm that official guidelines are in place, warning RAF and U.S. Air Force personnel not to discuss UFO sightings with the Press. They confirm the presence in our airspace of unknown objects of fantastic design and manoeuvrability; and they confirm that whatever UFOs are, they are considered to be a matter of extreme concern to the defence of both countries, if not the entire world.

Similarly, official files on the UFO subject are now surfacing from the governments of Russia, Italy, France, Australia, and Canada. Are we being slowly prepared for the day when the truth will finally be revealed? Perhaps; but until that day comes, however, I will continue my quest. As I was told by a former United States airman only six weeks ago: when they truth comes out, it's going to change the world overnight.

***

My second article for *The Weekender* went by the name of *Monsters Galore – The Exeter Files*. It was, of course, an utterly shameless plug for the good folk of the Centre for Fortean Zoology:

Space Girl Dead on Spaghetti Junction

Some children dream of being a rock star. Others have aspirations to be an astronaut, a racing-driver, or maybe even a famous actor. For Jonathan Downes, however, there was only ever one real dream: he wanted to be a monster hunter! As a child, Downes grew up in the wilds of Hong Kong and was exposed to all manner of exotic wildlife from an early age.

> 'My mother bought me a book on unknown animals at the time that was full of things like the Loch Ness Monster, Bigfoot, the Yeti and so on, and from that moment I was hooked!'

says the now-41-year-old Downes, from his home in Exwick, Exeter. Today, Downes is the director of the Centre for Fortean Zoolkogy (named after Charles Fort, an early chronicler of the mysteries of the world); and along with his colleagues Richard Freeman, and Graham Inglis, spends his life writing about, and pursuing, monsters across the globe. Having got well and truly tired of the world of 9-to-5, in 1994 Downes elected to make his dream come a reality and the CFZ was born. Today, Downes publishes two magazines on the subject of unknown creatures, has written a number of books, and is regularly consulted by the media.

He says:
> 'You would be surprised to learn how many weird reports there are of monsters and mysterious animals both in the U.K. and abroad. For example, here in Devonshire we have numerous reports of pumas and various other big cats on the loose. Indeed, I even saw one of these things myself a number of years ago, but to my everlasting regret, I failed to get a photograph of it.'

Downes' disappointment of the big-pussy kind didn't put paid to his investigations, however, and in 1998, he and Graham Inglis travelled out to the island of Puerto Rico with a Channel 4 television crew, in search of a vampire-like beast known as the Goat-Sucker that is rumoured to haunt the jungles of the island.

'To be honest,' Downes explains with good humour,
> 'I saw this as a bit of a break from the British weather! But when we got out there, we spoke with numerous farmers whose animals had been drained of blood by this creature and even police officers who had seen it. They described it as being like a kangaroo with vicious spikes on its back. I actually found the whole thing quite disturbing.'

Indeed, so strange was the story that Channel 4 devoted a one-hour, prime-time show to Downes and Inglis' exploits on the island. Similarly, Richard Freeman (formerly a head-keeper at Twycross Zoo) has just returned from an expedition to Thailand with a team from TV's Discovery Channel in search of a gigantic snake said to inhabit the Mekong River. Like a latter-day Indiana Jones, Freeman jumped at the chance to seek out the beast. That is not all: in a few months' time from now, the CFZ are off to the Gambia, in search of sea-serpents and a *Jurassic Park*-like dinosaur that allegedly lives in the heart of the jungle.

Space Girl Dead on Spaghetti Junction

For the Centre for Fortean Zoology, the lure of adventure is as important as any monster that they might actually uncover: 'I can imagine nothing worse,' says Jonathan Downes, 'than working in a job you hate and being told what to do by a boss you hate even more. What could be more fun than spending your life having adventures in exotic parts of the world, chasing monsters and, better still, getting paid for it?' Who could argue with that?

My final article for *The Weekender* was a profile on a woman named Jane Adams; a Leicester-based author who I ran into at a conference held at Walsall's College of Technology in 1999, at which I also met legendary horror-fiction author Guy N. Smith, who unintentionally reduced the entire audience to hysterics when, in his lecture, he referenced his novel *Crabs on the Rampage*! But, I digress, back to the feature:

Trying to earn a living from writing about the mysteries of the unexplained, whilst at the same time trying to maintain a normal family and social life can be a difficult experience at times – believe me, I know! However, one person who has managed to cope with all the madness that goes along with books, deadlines and the manic world of publishing is Leicester-based author and mother-of-two, Jane Adams. Jane is the author of six crime novels, all of which were published by the prestigious MacMillan Books, and she has a new title – *Like Angels Falling* – due for release in June 2001.

Prior to becoming a full-time writer, Jane had a variety of part-time jobs, including vocalist in a folk-rock band; a Tarot card reader; and a customer advisor in a building society. She has also acted in a research capacity for various writers on such subjects as UFOs, New Age spirituality, religious cults, and even whether men can fake orgasm! The jury, Jane says, is still out on the last one! But it was in 1995 that things really began to take off for Jane.

It was that year that saw the publication of her first novel – *The Greenway*. A book that mixed reality with the supernatural, *The Greenway* introduced a character (Detective Mike Croft) who would feature in future titles, and the book earned Jane nominations both for the *Crime Writers Association's John Creasey Award for Best First Crime Novel*; and also the *Authors Club Award for the Most Promising First Novel of 1995*.

Last year saw the beginning of a new series of titles from Jane that again blended the world as we know it with the realm of the unexplained. Jane's books are charged with atmosphere and transport the reader into what at times seem almost mystical worlds. *The Greenway*, for example, is a thought-provoking and chilling story of a young girl who disappears on an ancient pathway. Twenty years on, her cousin sets out to solve the mystery – only to find that another girl has disappeared. *Final Frame* is a book that takes the reader into the heart of the film world, death and the nature of evil itself; while *Bird* is an emotional rollercoaster of a ride. Indeed, all of Jane's books have been more than well-received. Jane's forthcoming title, *Like Angels Falling*, look set to continue that trend. Focusing on a sinister cult, ritualistic murders and much more, the book is sure to please Jane's fans and entice a whole new audience to pick up her books. Jane tells *The Weekender* that with a colleague, Gary William Murning, she has established Malkin Publications, which will be issuing a magazine titled *13*; an outlet for new fiction from authors writing in such genres as science-fiction, horror and crime that will be on sale on 22nd June.

Mothman Lives 2002

As many will recall, Mothman – which had previously been a bizarre critter obsessed over by the Fortean community and pretty much no-one else – became a household word in 2002, when Hollywood gave John Keel's *The Mothman Prophecies* book the cinematic, red-carpet treatment. I know a lot of people within the cryptozoological field utterly hated the film. But, I actually thought it was pretty good - and quite atmospheric, too. The film even prompted me to pen the following article, *In Search of the Mothman*, for the Walsall edition of the *Express & Star* newspaper:

If someone were to come up to you and inquire whether you had even seen a large, man-sized creature with bat-like wings and glowing red eyes, you might be inclined to smile nervously and slowly back away – and no-one would blame you. In a few short weeks, however, your response might be different. Mothman mania is about to hit the U.K. *The Mothman Prophecies* is a new Hollywood moving starring Richard Gere. It tells the story of dark and sinister goings-on in an American town. It involves everything from UFOs and Men in Black-style characters to monsters and things that go bump in the night. The film is a genuinely spooky look at a series of allegedly real events that occurred in Point Pleasant, West Virginia.

From November 1966 to December 1967, the entire area was beset by a wave of weirdness. People reported seeing strange lights in the sky above their homes, mysterious men would turn up on their doorsteps and warn them not to discuss what they had seen, frightening and nightmarish visions were commonplace and a sense of doom and dread enveloped the entire area when a nearby bridge collapsed killing dozens. And amidst all this small-town strangeness loomed the spectral presence of the Mothman. The events in question were investigated at the time by an acclaimed author on UFOs and the paranormal, John Keel, and ultimately published in his 1975 cult classic book, *The Mothman Prophecies*.

The film, however, updates things to the present day and tells the story of a Washington-based political journalist, John Klein (Gere), whose wife dies in tragic circumstances following a brief battle with a brain-tumour. In the wake of this tragedy, Klein, throwing himself into his work, heads for Point Pleasant in pursuit of a story, and inadvertently runs into a series of inexplicable events that would task even the best efforts of Mulder and Scully.

Thankfully, the film is not filled with scenes of a stuntman in a poorly-fitting moth suit flying shakily across the sky. Nor does it rely on shock-tactic-style special-effects to hammer home its story. Rather, *The Mothman Prophecies* focuses on atmosphere, shadowy locations and subtle imagery, and accurately portrays the sense of evil and impending doom that gripped the town of Point Pleasant at the time. Gere shines, too – trying to juggle with events in his personal life as he travels along a journey further and further into unreality.

What do UFOs, collapsing bridges, Men in Black and a gargoyle-like creature that looks like it walked off the set of *Jurassic Park*-meets-*Aliens* have in common? Well, while the film supplies the answers, I wouldn't dream of giving away the ending. Unlike most of the people who will be visiting their local cinema to see the film, however, for some, Mothman is nothing new.

Jonathan Downes is the director of the Exeter-based Centre for Fortean Zoology (named after Charles Fort, an early chronicler of all things mysterious) and, along with his sidekick, Richard Freeman, runs the only full-time monster hunting group in the U.K. For Downes and Freeman, every day is an adventure filled with sightings of big-cats on Dartmoor, Nessie, Bigfoot and a creepy-looking winged man rumoured to haunt the wilds of Cornwall – the Owlman! Admittedly obsessed by the Owlman, Downes has spent years and a small fortune pursuing it and interviewing people who claim to have seen this British equivalent of Point Pleasant's flying whatsit.

So how does Downes feel about the Mothman getting the big-time Hollywood treatment? Shouldn't Britain's very own version be getting the royal treatment, too? 'Indeed, he should,' says Downes. 'I'm looking forward to seeing the film and hope they capture the spirit of the story. But, perhaps, one day Britain's Owlman will be as famous as Mothman is about to become.'

And who would portray the 6ft 6ins Downes, whose resemblance to Bigfoot is beyond startling?

'My dear boy,' he tells me, 'I am unique among men. I would have to play myself. Hollywood: are you listening?'

If *The Mothman Prophecies* lives up to all the hype, Jonathan Downes may well indeed one day see his face up on the silver-screen. Now, that *would* be scary.

A Conference, a Camera, a Conspiracy 2003

In November 2003, Roswell/MJ12 researcher Ryan Wood, for whom I had then been working for two-years in what was pretty much a full-time capacity, held the first of a still-on-going series of gigs in Las Vegas, Nevada on all-things crashed and saucer-shaped: the *UFO Crash-Retrieval Conference* was well and truly born. Somewhat appropriately - given the fact that both Jon Downes, and crop-circle-maker, and underground-base-invader, Matthew Williams spoke at the event – the premier gig proved to be highly surreal, controversial and downright conspiratorial in nature. On returning home from that weekend of absolute debauchery, I quickly wrote up the nature of the event; lest it drift into overwhelming obscurity, as a result of my alcohol-soaked few days deep in the heart of Sin-City itself. Unfortunately, after I had prepared my report on the distinctly strange saga, I quickly realized that it simply didn't really have relevance to anything else I was working on at the time. The result: it merely languished in obscurity on my hard-drive...until now, of course. But, today, the time is right to unleash my written recollections of November 2003 upon an unsuspecting world. And here it is; an enigmatic, strange and *News of the World*-worthy tale of truly definitive 'what happens in Vegas stays in Vegas' proportions:

Little did I know that what was planned as a relatively normal and perhaps, to some, even bland, UFO conference in Las Vegas in November 2003, would ultimately turn out be something far stranger, and would subsequently be talked about in hushed tones for years afterwards in places where the flying saucer faithful gather. In early

2003, Ryan Wood phoned me and explained that he had decided to hold a conference at Las Vegas on the controversial subject of crashed UFOs. He envisaged making it a yearly event (which it did subsequently become – and a highly successful one, too), where those with a particular interest in crashed UFO stories could gather and learn the latest on Roswell, the alien autopsy film, Area 51, and much more.

Ryan asked me: "Do you have any ideas as to who we could get on board to speak at the conference?" I did, indeed. My first task was to pick up the telephone and call two of my oldest and closest mates back in Britain – Matthew Williams and Jonathan Downes. I had known Wales-born Matthew since 1994, and at a time when both of us were looking into allegations of high-level, official UFO investigations undertaken by the British military at a Royal Air Force base in the southwest of England called RAF Rudloe Manor. The base was certainly an unusual one and sat atop a futuristic, underground installation, and a veritable rabbit warren of tunnels that resembled something straight out of an *Austin Powers*-style parody of a *James Bond* movie.

I got on very well with Matt (we shared the same obscure, somewhat dark, sense of humour and were both devotees of H.P. Lovecraft) and we spent a lot of time in the mid-to-late 1990s travelling around the United Kingdom together, speaking at a range of gigs, and investigating varied and sundry government chicanery with respect to the weird world of the unidentified flying object.

Although Matt was widely known and respected on the British UFO research scene throughout much of the 1990s, it was in the latter part of 2000 that he really arrived when he became the first (and, to date, *the only*) person ever arrested, charged, and ultimately convicted by the British Police Force for making a crop circle; or, more correctly, one of the more elaborate Pictograms. While the official charge against Matt was one of "causing criminal damage to private property," no one – and certainly least of all the nation's frenzied media that gleefully covered the ridiculous and farcical court case in every detail – cared a damn about the official stance. Matt was forever immortalized in the country's eyes as the world's only convicted crop circle hoaxer.

The fact that Matt had merely constructed the formation because some armchair theorists were saying that such a thing could not possibly be undertaken and executed by human hand under cover of darkness – and Matt was determined to conduct a scientific experiment to prove them wrong – was largely ignored. Matt's actions provoked violent fury in some quarters, and envy and admiration in others. For me, it was business as usual: Matt was a good mate and we both laughed – and still do – about the absurdity of the whole affair, that saw him pursued, in true Beatlemania style, by Britain's press.

But back to the Vegas gig: I outlined the theme of the conference to Matt, who offered to deliver a lecture on two subjects that I knew would instantly have Ryan salivating. Specifically, Matt would: (a) disclose his never-before-seen findings on allegations that an unspecified number of alien corpses were held in a cryogenic facility deep below the cavernous RAF Rudloe Manor; and (b) reveal the details of an extensive interview he had undertaken in 1997 with a teenaged, Welsh computer hacker named Matthew Bevan, who, in 1994, had actually succeeded in penetrating the heart of Wright-Patterson Air Force Base's computer system. Incredibly, Bevan had uncovered copious amounts of highly classified data on a very strange "anti-gravity"-style aircraft that was rumoured to be back-engineered from the remains of a crashed UFO that was housed in a secure, underground facility at the base.

The Bevan caper was a genuinely strange one, with Scotland Yard, the FBI, the CIA, and even Chinese Military Intelligence all closely watching the seventeen-year-old computer hacker and tracking his every move. Unlike the situation with Matt, attempts to prosecute Bevan collapsed when the U.S. Government curiously dropped the charges and Bevan was free to sell his story to Britain's most notorious tabloid newspaper, *The News of the World* - which he quickly did, and for a tidy sum of cash. Who says crime doesn't pay? If you are a teenaged computer hacker looking for dead aliens and spacecraft with anti-gravity drives, it certainly does.

As I predicted, Ryan was immediately sold on the idea. Next stop, the Lord of the Manor himself: Sir Jonathan of Downeshire. In 1998, Jon had travelled to the heart of Puerto Rico in search of a weird, vampire-like beast alleged by many to resemble a diabolical cross between a monkey, a hyena, a gargoyle, and a stereotypical, black-eyed, bald-headed alien, and that would become universally known as the Chupacabras.

While the Chupacabras had little – if, indeed, anything – to do with crashed UFOs, I knew that while he was on the island, Jon had gathered numerous tales relating to a crashed UFO incident that had reportedly occurred deep within the darkened depths of Puerto Rico's El Yunque rain forest at some not-entirely-determined point in the mid-1980s. Could Jon deliver a picture-driven lecture that would reveal all to what would hopefully be a wide-eyed and awe-struck audience?

"Of course I can, dear boy!" he absolutely bellowed down the phone. The game was afoot, as Holmes was fond of remarking to his special friend, Watson. Ryan booked the flight-tickets and reserved the hotel-rooms, and the three musketeers were about to hit Vegas. It was November 14, 2003, and I flew into Vegas' McCarran International Airport around 3.00 p.m., and waited for Jon and Matt to arrive, as their flight from England was due to land in barely ninety minutes time. Luckily they were on schedule, and we were soon catching up on old times in one of the airport's bars.

We had roughly an hour-and-a-half to kill before our shuttle bus arrived, and so, after having sunk a few pints and having found an abandoned airport-wheelchair, Jon and I entertained ourselves by pushing Matt around the airport while he, pretending to be of less than sound mind, ranted and screamed at anyone and everyone within twenty feet of us. We explained to the astonished onlookers that Matt was our deranged, in-bred younger brother, and that it was not his fault he was utterly insane. Needless to say, we received very little in the form of sympathy.

We finally got to the hotel, the *Sunset Station Casino* at the nearby town of Henderson, around

Space Girl Dead on Spaghetti Junction

6.00 p.m., ate, drank, caught up with old friends and colleagues like Peter Robbins, Greg Bishop, and Kenn Thomas, and then wandered around the hotel looking for some entertainment. That entertainment - and I use the term sparingly - turned out to be an incredibly boring cover-band that played nothing but 1980s hairspray heavy-metal from such dreadful stalwarts of that era as *Quiet Riot, Poison, Winger,* and *Ratt*. It was great fun to watch – but for all of the wrong reasons. And so, after an hour or two of synchronized head banging, and long discussions about Flying-V guitars, silver spandex, and ridiculous hairstyles we headed for our respective rooms. But not before having a drink in the bar with a guy who I will call "Bill;" and who had travelled all the way from South America.

Despite the fact that Jon scoffed at much of the paranoia and the claims of cover-up and conspiracy that abounded within the UFO field, even he had come to the same conclusion that Matt and I had: that Bill was some sort of deep-cover spook type whose attendance at the conference was in an official capacity, no less. Indeed, Bill's big business activities in South America and his links with some highly influential people and companies almost shouted out: CIA Station-Officer. But, admittedly, he was a fun guy to hang out with, and we had a riotous time at the bar discussing all things ufological and crypto-zoological.

For most of the next day, aside from when we were lecturing, me, Jon and Matt seemed to spend our time trying to avoid a very strange, ultra-racist character who shuffled around in clothes that stunk like an open sewer, and who insisted on ranting at us about his theories concerning the moon-landings (faked), Roswell (real), the JFK assassination (the work of Russian time-travellers), and the Loch Ness Monster (the demonic creation of Aleister Crowley). At first we tried to be polite, but, whenever we disagreed with him, we were in return faced with a barrage of insults, and so we finally, and less-than-politely, told him to go and screw himself. He may well have done so, since we never saw him again. Or, perhaps, Bill had him fatally dealt in the fashion that only a covert CIA spook truly, and fatally, can.

I may be biased, but for me the most entertaining lecture of the day was Jon's. While everyone else, myself included, I confess, gave longwinded lectures on everything ufological and crashed, Jon spent his time telling the bemused audience about (a) how much Tequila he had managed to down while on Puerto Rico; (b) how he had managed to massively inflate his expense sheet with the TV company that had hired him; (c) his nefarious adventures smuggling rare snails through Puerto Rican Customs at San Juan Airport; and (d) the sexual activities of the island's lesser-spotted great newt – or some such similarly weird creature, anyway.

Finally he got to the crashed UFO story; but I forget now what all the fuss was about. But I do recall that the story involved a spaceship that had hurtled to the ground in the El Yunque rain forest, an area of land that had been cordoned off by the U.S. military, and the removal by that same U.S. military of the object and its crew of diminutive, bald-headed, black-eyed aliens. The usual Mulder and Scully fodder, in other words.

So far, it was just any normal UFO conference. But it was around about 8.00 p.m. that things began to change. I, Matt, Jon, Bill and a few others all got down to the banquet room earlier than the rest of the crowd, so that we could grab a table and all sit together. And a fine time was had by all of us, as we dined and drank to an outrageous extent, and all at the expense of the good Ryan. Then it was time for the after-dinner speech; from UFO researcher Michael Lindemann, who, at one point, a drunken Matthew approached, and loudly proclaimed: "You look like Steve Austin. You know: the *Six Million Dollar Man*." A somewhat bemused Michael merely smiled politely and said nothing.

As we sat and listened to Michael (on what particular subject, I have no idea now), I felt a sudden feeling of vertigo come over me. Okay, I had had a few drinks; but not *that* many. Then I felt the uncontrollable urge to laugh – and laugh manically and hysterically, but at absolutely nothing at all. Five minutes later, Jon began to do exactly the same. Overwhelming paranoia seemed to set in, and the room seemed to be moving ever so slightly. Colours seemed brighter and more vivid than normal, and I imagined that something diabolically evil was lurking within the depths of my whisky-and-coke. In the words of the *Ramones*' song of 1986: *Somebody Put Something in my Drink*; and in Jon's glass, too.

Indeed, such was the strange condition that we were in Jon and I were forced to leave the room, laughing manically and in sinister fashion, as we headed in less than steady fashion for the elevators and the post-conference party that was just about to start in one of the rooms upstairs. Most of the speakers ultimately arrived, as well as a few hangers-on, and whose faces seemed to take on crazed expressions of terror whenever I looked at them. Also present was Jim Moseley, the infamous and legendary editor of the gossip magazine *Saucer Smear*, and ufological hero par excellence. Matt arrived shortly afterwards, and still suffering from jetlag, promptly passed out on the bed for the rest of the night. The air was soon thick with the smell of high-quality marijuana.

Jim asked me if I would take some pictures of him with all of the speakers, which, despite my befuddled and paranoid state, I said I would be happy to do. I shot perhaps twelve pictures, and placed Jim's camera on the table. However, when Jim came to change the camera's film, it was curiously missing. It was gone; vanished. Everyone was baffled, and Jim particularly was flummoxed.

As I had been the last person to take pictures with the camera in question, I inevitably became suspect number one. In the March 2004 issue of Jim's newsletter, *Saucer Smear*, he reproduced a letter from Greg Bishop that read:

> "For awhile I thought you were angry with me for the mysterious film disappearance episode during my party at the Las Vegas (Henderson, Nevada) party. You didn't even mention my (or Kenn Thomas') name as the host. Who do you think was responsible? Have you seen the piece examining that fateful night that Grant Cameron put up on the (cursed) net? I'm glad to finally be accused of being an evil government agent!" In response to Greg's letter, Jim added: "We are 99.9% sure that the villain in this 'mysterious' but trivial film incident was none other than Nick Redfern."

The rest of the evening was a veritable blur, with ever more paranoid tales about missing cameras, CIA spooks, mind-control, and mysterious deaths dominating the conversation. I finally began to feel not too well at all, and stumbled back to my room and passed out fully clothed on the bed. The next day, however, I felt fine, and the odd sensations and the strange atmosphere of the previous night were all absent. I ran into Jim in the lobby and asked him if he had found his camera film. He eyed me suspiciously, and replied that, no, he had not. I promised to send him copies of my own pictures that I had taken at the conference when I got home, and his face changed, and a broad smile beamed forth. Indeed, after returning to Dallas, I did as promised and received a nice letter of thanks from Jim in return. But, even to this very day, I still get asked questions about that weird night of spooks, psychedelic substances, and stolen celluloid.

Later on that afternoon, me, Jon, Matt, Greg and Kenn all crammed into the little car that Greg had hired for the weekend, and we headed off for a night of fun in the Nevada desert. We loaded the car with snacks and booze, and Greg entertained us with a fine and eclectic selection of CDs. I am not sure where we went exactly, but it was deep into the heart of the wilderness, and we spent a glorious couple of hours communing with nature, and relaxing to the magical qualities that all deserts seem to possess. But, we had to get back as there was another party planned – in Ryan's room, and as a thank-you to all of the speakers.

This time it was a rather more staid affair than that of the night before. There was no missing camera film and no psychotic episodes. At around midnight, we all said our goodbyes and got ready for a trip back to the airport early on Monday morning. Unfortunately, Matt had to head back to England. Jon, however, had decided to stay in the States for an extra week, and flew back to Nederland with me, where he hung out with us for the next seven days, eating Gumbo and rampaging wildly, whiskey bottle in hand, around darkened woods in hot pursuit of the Texas Bigfoot. But the journey back to Nederland was not the uneventful trip that we had envisaged. I suppose we should have guessed: nothing in our lives was ever uneventful.

As soon as we got to our departure lounge for our flight that was scheduled for 1.15 p.m., we learned that it had been delayed due to bad weather near Houston Airport. As the day progressed the delays got longer and sheer boredom set in; so, Jon and I decided to play a little game. Every time someone sat next to us, Jon would pull out his cell-phone, put on a pair of wrap-around sun-glasses, turn up the collar of his dark jacket, and look around the room in a distinctly cloak-and-dagger fashion, and whisper into his phone just loud enough for the person to hear him say:

> "Condition red, condition red. The Black Condor has landed. I repeat: the Black Condor has landed. Alert all personnel to move in, and terminate with extreme prejudice."

It was my job to judge the reaction of the person who was the subject of our utterly mindless mind-games. Invariably, we were treated with looks of disgust. Doubtless they were not amused by the sight of two men, one in his thirties (me), and the other in his forties (Jon) playing completely inane, but highly entertaining, games when they really should by now have grown out of such nonsense. The tiring and stressed-out world of adulthood and the attendant responsibilities of kids, mortgages, real jobs and other such utterly mystifying oddities were not for us, however.

As the cell phone caper continued and the hours rolled by, occasionally we would lure in some unsuspecting and gullible soul who fell for our prank. Worried, furtive looks would be cast in our direction, whispered conversations with their partners would follow, and they would then get up and move to another seat, while still watching us intently, though. But, finally, even we got bored and laid the Black Condor to rest.

Five hours after we were originally due to fly, we were still stuck at the accursed airport. Then, at 7.00 p.m., an announcement was made that the weather had improved slightly near Houston, and a decision had been made "to attempt the flight." It was that particularly unusual phraseology that caused many people within the terminal to take on worried frowns. And it was not unwarranted. As we took off from Vegas around 9.00 p.m. at night, everything started fine, and Jon and me settled back into our respective seats, ate a pleasant dinner, and downed a few drinks. But as the aircraft neared Texas, the weather began to get steadily worse again, to the point where we were literally being buffeted around the sky; and lightning, thunder, and driving rain became our constant and only companions.

On two occasions the interior lights momentarily went out – amid hysterical screams that emanated from all around the aircraft – and the ominous creaking and groaning of metal could be heard from time to time. Jon closed his eyes, and began to pray out loud to a whole assortment of ancient deities. But it was his bellowing, whisky-driven plea to "the beasts of old England" to get us on the ground in one piece that really shook up the people that were sat across the aisle from us. Here we were, 40,000 feet in the air, in the middle of probably the worst flight that most of us had ever experienced, and Jon was invoking shadowy beings from Britain's dark forests in an attempt to assist the captain and crew as they struggled to keep the plane in the air, and subsequently get us on the ground in one piece. And finally, we *were* on the ground – and in that much welcome one piece, too. In a fashion surreally similar to one of those old aircraft disaster movies of the 1970s, everyone cheered and clapped when we finally came to a halt, and we all disembarked; many I suspect, with distinctly shaky legs.

But we were still not out of the woods: I phoned Dana when we finally got off the plane around midnight, and she told me that numerous trees had come down on the main highway to Houston from Nederland, and the road was blocked. Not only that: the ongoing storm meant that trees were still coming down, so I told her not to attempt the 90-minute car journey alone at the witching hour. Instead, Jon and I settled down in the terminal for a night on the floor, with our carry-on luggage substituting for pillows. It was a torturous seven hours. But dawn finally broke, and we got a flight to Nederland and were soon sprawled on our living room couch devouring gumbo and drinking a fine bottle of red wine.

It was the first time that Jon and Dana had seen each other since her visit to England in May 2001, and we had a good time catching up on gossip and telling stories, while Charity sniffed, and stared intently at, her grizzly-bear-like visitor from across the ocean. The next day, I drove Jon, with Charity pacing excitedly on the backseat, around the swamps in search of alligators, snakes and road-kill – and, fortunately, he got to see and photograph all three. But it was the following day that, I suspect, was Jon's favorite.

Only a few miles from Nederland was the town of Orange, where renowned crypto-zoologist Chester Moore lived. I had met first Chester in the summer of 2003 at his Crypto Conference in Conroe, Texas. Several days before I flew to Vegas, I had phoned Chester to tell him that Jon was coming over, and he was eager to arrange a meeting. So, I called Chester again, and he drove over, and Jon and me spent the day with him exploring the woods of East Texas and visiting various places where giant, hairy behemoths had been seen roaming – and by that I do not mean Jon. But first we paid a visit to Chester's home and where he showed us around his office – that was packed with Bigfoot footprint casts, crypto-related movie posters, and, incredibly, a life-sized replica of Bigfoot himself that Chester had christened "Boggy." The model had apparently got its name from the 1973 movie, *The Legend of Boggy Creek* that told the story of a series of man-beast encounters in the early 1970s at Fouke, Arkansas.

Seeing Jon stood next to the beast, as I took a few photographs, momentarily flummoxed me, as the resemblance between the two was uncannily remarkable. Indeed, they could have almost been twins. And then it was time to hit the road.

The good thing about investigating cryptids in East Texas is the fact that a person does not have to venture far off the main highways before they are deep into the woods. And having done so, Chester told us some amazing stories about the unholy sounds (or "vocalizations" as he preferred it) that he had heard from deep within the woods late at night that he was firmly convinced originated with the creature known as Bigfoot. Footprints abounded, he said, and there was no doubt that something monstrous was lurking deep inside the sinister woods.

We didn't see the creature, mind you, but both Jon and I were convinced of the veracity and credibility of Chester's research. After Chester dropped us off back at our house, we said our collective goodbyes; and then with Dana, headed out for an evening of fine food and good conversation. But after a couple of more days of relaxation it was time for Jon to begin his journey back to England, and for me and Dana to plan our next adventure – a move to the big city of Dallas.

Me and Downesy, loitering with intent.

In Search of the Chupacabras - New Revelations 2005

Back in mid 2004, Jon Downes and I spent a week charging wildly around Puerto Rico in crazed fashion, in search of the diabolical Chupacabras – while fueled on fine food, margaritas and a significant amount of adrenalin – and all to the mighty tones of *Sham 69* that boomed out of the speakers of a silver-jeep that the SyFy Channel had the good taste to hire for us for the week. Well, on returning home to Dallas, Texas, I happened to mention details of our excursion to Phyliis Galde, the editor of *Fate* magazine, who enthusiastically asked for an article on the subject for her publication, which I was pleased to pen, in 2005, titled *In Search of the Chupacabras: New Revelations*:

In July 2004, I travelled to the island of Puerto Rico for a week with fellow cryptozoologist, good friend, and director of the British-based Center for Fortean Zoology, Jonathan Downes, and a production team from the Sci-Fi Channel's new *Proof Positive* television series. The purpose of our trip was to make a 20-minute segment for *Proof Positive* on the still-on-going mystery of the diabolical Chupacabras. To say that our excursion to the island was an extraordinary one would most definitely not be an understatement.

This was my first visit to Puerto Rico to specifically look for the elusive beast. Jon, however, had undertaken a similar quest in 1998 with a British television crew and had seen firsthand both the horrific, physical handiwork of the creature and the psychological and financial effects that the Chupacabras attacks had on the local populace.

Indeed, until a person actually spends time travelling the island and personally speaking with witnesses, government employees, police officers and ranchers (all of who have been implicated in the mystery to varying degrees), it is incredibly difficult to appreciate the sheer scale of the way in which the Chupacabras mystery has become so ingrained in Puerto Rican society. Not only that: despite the fact that it was during the mid-to-late 1990s that the Chupacabras phenomenon was at its height, attacks are still regularly occurring, even if people are somewhat reluctant to report or discuss such incidents.

We quite literally travelled the length and breadth of the island on our weeklong journey of discovery and interviewed numerous ranchers whose animals (including chickens, cows, pigs and even peacocks) had been found slaughtered and whose deaths had been attributed to the Chupacabras. Typically, two small puncture wounds were found on the necks of practically all of the animals in question; massive amounts of blood had been drained from their bodies with fantastic speed; and major, bodily organs had been removed, sometimes with incredible and disturbing precision.

In one particularly notable case, we spoke in-depth with a farmer whose chickens had been mutilated and killed during the hours of darkness in this precise fashion. What made this incident stand out more than any other as being particularly unusual, however, was the fact that whatever had killed the chickens had first carefully and quietly opened the complex locks on each of the cages in which the animals were held. To all of us, this suggested a sophisticated degree of cunning, intelligence and dexterity at work.

The other case that really stood out as being of prime significance involved a lady who lived in a property that overlooked the incredibly beautiful El Yunque rain forest of Puerto Rico and who had what was quite literally a face-to-face encounter with the Chupacabras in 1975. She would describe the animal as being approximately four-feet in height, and having a monkey-like body that was covered in hair or fur that was dark brown in colour, wings that were a cross between those of a bat and those of a bird, glowing eyes that bulged from a bat-style face, and fingers with sharp, claw-like appendages. Whatever the creature was, it left a deep, lasting impression upon the woman, who recalled the near-30-year-old encounter as if it had occurred only yesterday.

For a week we travelled across Puerto Rico, headed deep into the El Yunque rain forest and the caves of the island, and spoke with countless witnesses to the creature and its deadly habits. At the end of our foray into the world of the Chupacabras, I could only come to one conclusion: regardless of the many theories that have been postulated concerning the origin of the creature, the Chupacabras is a very real animal and a very dangerous one, too.

In one of life's ironies, what was perhaps the most notable account that I uncovered on the Chupacabras mystery came not during the shoot with the *Proof Positive* team, but a week later and was provided by a lead from one of the interviewees we had made friends with on the island of Puerto Rico. In a lengthy telephone conversation after I had returned home to Dallas, I was able to speak with a lady named Rosa, who had a remarkable tale to tell and who was an acquaintance of the aforementioned interviewee.

It was 1991 and Rosa – who works in a small restaurant on the island - was driving home with a friend after a night in San Juan. For a reason that to this day Rosa is unable to determine, both she and her friend felt compelled to drive their car high into the El Yunque rain forest – which was something, Rosa explained, she would never have normally done and certainly not at 1.00 a.m. on a Saturday morning.

Nevertheless, the pair duly headed along the snaking roads that lead up to the forest and were confronted by a horrific sight as they rounded one particular bend: a four-to-five-foot-tall animal that crossed the road in front of them at a distance of about fifty to sixty feet and in a manner that was described to me as an awkward, shuffling gait. The creature appeared to be very dark gray in colour and had two large wings that seemed to be wrapped around its back (and that gave the appearance of a long cloak) and that dragged on the surface of the road as it walked.

Rosa stated that both she and her friend were terrified by the presence of the beast and watched in horror as it continued to very slowly cross the road. Rosa added that the creature even glared at them for a split second with a pair of what appeared to be self-illuminating, glowing red eyes. Too shocked to do anything than stare in awe, the pair continued to watch as the animal shuffled into the trees and bushes and was lost from sight.

Thirteen years after her experience, Rosa spoke in a nervous voice as she related her account to me. Other than telling her family and several close friends (one being a friend of one of the interviewees encountered during our summer 2004 visit to Puerto Rico), Rosa informed me that she had discussed the encounter with no one. However, for Rosa the most bizarre aspect of the encounter was not the sighting itself, but the fact that she is of the opinion to this day that the creature somehow impelled her to drive to the El Yunque rain forest with the express intention of ensuring that she saw it – for purposes that neither I nor she can adequately determine. If nothing else, it demonstrates that the mystery of the Chupacabras is a truly strange one. And things do not end there.

In early December 2004, no less than eleven goats were found slaughtered inside their wooden pen at the Illusion children's park in Rio Piedras, Puerto Rico. The discovery had been made by the owner of the park's petting zoo: Fausto Radaelli. According to the explanation given by Radaelli, he had taken the goats to the park the previous Monday, with the intention of recreating "a manger scene for the Christmas holiday." Two days later, however, the animals were dead.

The *Primera Hora* newspaper of December 3 stated:

> "Three of the goats presented large bite marks, dismemberment and one of them had half of its body devoured; all of its internal organs, excepting its stomach, were gone. The rest of the goats had bite marks and fang marks on the rear of their bodies. The marks resembled the ones found on animals allegedly attacked by the infamous Chupacabras."

> However, Ernesto Marquez, a biologist and a specialist in exotic animals, concluded that the goats were attacked by "a wolf, a coyote, a hybrid or very large feral dogs...these are regular fang marks. Canids kill animals by the rear, seizing them to hold them down and eat them. The animal leaped; it is an agile animal, attacking from the rear. It's astute and knows human beings. This is vicious. The animal isn't psychologically well."

The site was also examined by both Julio Diaz of the Animal Control Solutions Company, and veterinary technician Herman Sulsona of the San Juan Animal Control Center. Notably, although Ernesto Marquez was convinced that the killings had a down-to-earth explanation, there were no signs of forcible entry in the pen, and more intriguingly, *no prints or hairs of any other animal aside from the goats themselves were found.*

Moving away from the world of fact to the realm of fiction, a new movie on the Chupacabras that is scheduled to appear later this year is already making big waves and is sure to further intensify the debate surrounding the mysterious beast.

Titled *Cabras*, the movie is the first in a trilogy of productions on the Chupacabras to be made by Polania Pictures. Thanks to the Assistant Producer on the movie, Monica Polania, in December 2004 I was able to conduct an exclusive interview with the Director, Producer, Cinematographer and Editor of *Cabras*, Fredy Polania, who stated that:

> "If I were to classify the movie in a short description, I would say that it is *The Exorcist* meets *The Texas Chainsaw Massacre*."

Polania added:

> "I was born of Colombian parents who resided in Napa, California for 18 years, and the world of cinema has inspired me ever since I was a child. And I guess what really got me involved in filmmaking was the director Francis Ford Coppola, who also lives in Napa. His way of making movies really taught me a true sense of what I call guerilla filmmaking."

And what was it that prompted Polania to cross paths with Puerto Rico's notoriously ferocious beast?

Polania explained:

> "The unknown has always intrigued me. The mysteries behind such things as crop circles, spirits, and paranormal activities led me to look at the Chupacabras. There are so many questions: Is it a beast? Is it a demon? Does it have an alien source? Or, is it even possibly the devil, himself? And how can one entity cause so much havoc and never get captured? For the past fifteen years, the mutilations and deaths have terrorized us. And so our story begins."

Polania expanded further on his desire to document the mystery of the Chupacabras:

> "Let me ask you this: When you stare in a dark room and you see things, you ask yourself: 'Is it really there?' And to most people, the mystery behind the Chupacabras is in their minds. But the proof is here. The animal mutilations alone are proof – to me - that this is something extraterrestrial. Personally, I believe it's real. I think it's waiting to reveal itself. But why it hasn't already, I don't know. But there is something out there far beyond what we can even imagine. My belief is that the Chupacabras is extraterrestrial; but I also believe that there is something much higher to this - maybe spiritual, maybe biblical, even. And it *is* said that at the end of time a beast would walk the earth."

Intriguing words, indeed.

Polania had equally intriguing comments to make on the way in which the cast and crew came together on the movie:

> "Before a single shot was ever even captured, I had put together a crew; but not by the usual way of placing ads in newspapers. It had to be something much more special and I put together the crew through my own intuition. And what we found was that the movie started to manifest itself. I call my crew my research team, as they are something much more than just a crew. Beginning in the summer of 2000, we traveled to different parts of the world and took eyewitness accounts and collected stories from people. What we found shocked us. I can tell you that the world has been going about this the wrong way. If people knew what was *really* going on out there, they would not treat the Chupacabras as a joke."

In similar vein, Polania stated: "The cast feel like they've done this already and it's almost as if we've all met before and as if we were brought together by fate. In fact, the way we all connected was almost as if we were brought together by something greater."

I asked Polania how he thought the movie would be viewed and interpreted by those with an interest in the Chupacabras mystery as well as by the general public and the media. Would it be perceived as just another standard horror movie? Polania was unequivocal in his views:

> "I think this movie is going to be an eye opener. I want to stress that *Cabras* is *not* a movie about death. It's a movie about something that lives amongst us. I think that with our movie the public will find a new perspective on what the paranormal is really about."

"Is this going to be shown in theaters or is it going to be a movie for people to buy or rent as a video or DVD?" I inquired.

"The movie's trailers have already been seen in over 120 countries worldwide," Polania revealed.

> "The response has been astronomical. Even before it's been officially released, the movie is becoming almost like a cult: the truth, the legend, the beginning. I feel this movie is too complex for it to go straight to DVD. We are currently negotiating a domestic theatre release. This is actually a three-movie series and I want the beginning of the story to be shown the right way."

Polania added:

> "The official website of the movie is online right now – at www.cabrasmovie.com - and people can learn more about it there. But in a few months' time - and closer to the release date of the movie - we will unleash behind-the-scenes footage, interviews, eyewitness accounts, and an interactive forum. Regarding the release, it will be towards the end of 2005. You'll find that the next few films to be released by Polania Pictures will all be supernaturally based."

On the subject of Polania Pictures, he explained to me that: "Our crew is quite small. Our philosophy is that you don't need a million dollars to make a great film. The company is based on the trust of friends and it is the love of movies that brought us all together. We all dedicated four years of our lives with no pay to make this movie. The movie could never have been done without the closeness and trust we had in each other. *Cabras* is the first film from this group of friends and family."

Fredy Polania stated in closing: "This is something I was born to do. The unknown and the mystery of it is something I have to tell. And: what better way than in a movie?"

What better way, indeed? Look out for *Cabras* at a theatre near you later this year. Whatever the true nature of the Chupacabras, both off-screen and on-screen it seems that the exploits of the creature are certain to continue.

Enter the Dragon Hunter 2006

Whenever any of my mates have a new book published, I always try and give them some good publicity. Such was the case in 2005, when *Dragons: More Than A Myth?* penned by Little Dickie Freeman (or Richard Freeman, the world's only gothic cryptozoologist, as the man himself prefers it) reared its monstrous head. My article, titled *Enter the Dragon Hunter* - was splashed across a variety of blogs, magazines and websites – several of which are still operating; but many of which are long-gone. Fortunately, my original Word document still clings tenaciously to life! And here's the evidence to prove it:

Four teenage boys are brutally dragged to their deaths by a reptilian monster that emerges from a fog-bound sea off the coast of Florida. In the north-east of England, a shadowy cult is rumored to have sacrificed human victims to a dragon-god well into the 20th Century. In New Guinea, marauding giant lizards with huge teeth and vicious claws mercilessly slaughter dozens of villagers and send the natives into a panic. In the Gambia, an enraged dragon destroys a bridge, tipping people to their doom.

From childhood we are taught that dragons are nothing more than imaginary beasts – the things of fantasy, myth and legend. Indeed, the accounts cited above all sound like the perfect scripts for the wildest of Hollywood movies. According to full-time cryptozoologist and former zoo-keeper Richard Freeman, however, the legends are all-too-real. Moreover, the events cited above all occurred well within living memory.

While many monster-hunters are content to focus their attentions on Bigfoot, the Yeti, and the Loch Ness Monster, Freeman has spent the last decade doggedly and devotedly traveling the world in hot pursuit of real-life dragons – the amazing results of which are now available for one and all to read in his book new book *Dragons: More Than a Myth?*

In a moment we will take a strange trip into the unknown, where, deep in the shadows and the jungles, beasts such as the Naga, Mokele-mbembe, and Megalania lurk. But first, some essential background on what is that makes a man a dragon-hunter.

As a young boy growing up in England in the 1970s, Freeman regularly holidayed with his grandparents in the picturesque county of Devon – where Sir Arthur Conan Doyle's classic novel, *The Hound of the Baskervilles*, was set. One summer, when he was nine, Freeman watched and listened with awe and excitement when his grandfather got talking to a retired fisherman in Goodrington Harbor and who had a startling tale to relate.

Several years earlier the fisherman and his crew were trawling off of Berry Head, where the seas of Britain are almost at their deepest. Indeed, such are the depths of this part of the English Channel that the area is commonly used as a graveyard for old ships, and the drowned wrecks of these once-mighty vessels have made an artificial reef that has attracted vast amounts of fish.

On one particular moonlit night, the crew had trouble lifting the nets and began to worry that they had gotten entwined around the remains of a rotting, ship's mast. Soon, however, they felt some slack and duly began to haul the nets up. The men thought that their catch was a particularly good one, so heavy were their nets. As the nets drew closer to the trawler's lights, however, a frightening and diabolical sight took shape. The crew had not caught hundreds of normal-sized fish, but one gigantic creature.

The old fisherman quietly told Freeman's grandfather: "It was an eel, a giant eel. Its mouth was huge, wide enough to have swallowed a man; the teeth were as long as my hand." Even today, more than a quarter of a century later, Freeman still remembers the words of the ancient mariner and is convinced that this was not a tall story designed to entertain gullible tourists.

"While it was still in the water," added the fisherman,

> "it was buoyed up, but as soon as we tried to pull it onboard the nets snapped like cotton and it vanished back down. I was glad it went. I've been at sea all my life but I've never been as scared as I was that night. I can still see its eyes, huge glassy."

And from that moment on, the life of Richard Freeman was forever changed and the dragon-hunter began to take shape.

For three years Freeman worked as Head of Reptiles at Twycross Zoo, England and, today, is the Zoological Director of one of the world's premier cryptozoological investigation groups: namely, the Center for Fortean Zoology. And while Freeman has a passion for all aspects of cryptozoolgy, it is the dragon that fascinates him most of all, as he told me in August 2006 when we were both lecturing at the British-based *Weird Weekend* conference – an annual event that covers everything from UFOs to Crop Circles, Bigfoot to life-after-death, and just about anything and everything else in between.

Richard Freeman, Goth-Lord and Crypto Dude.

"I started my career as a zoologist – so I had a grounded training," says Freeman.

> "But cryptozoology was my passion. Now, I have had a particular passion – an obsession, I suppose – for years with dragons. But there was something that always puzzled me: no-one had ever thought, for more than a hundred years, to publish a definitive, non-fiction book on the subject. And I thought: why not me?"

Why not, indeed? I asked Freeman about his theories and discoveries with regard to dragons. He replied:

> "Well, that's a bit difficult to answer because there are several things going on. It's important to note that I've travelled the world pursuing these creatures – the Gambia, Mongolia, Thailand, and right here in England with some of the old legends from past centuries. And of one thing I can be certain: there isn't just one answer to the question of what dragons are or what they may be."

Freeman continued:

> "There are many creatures that have become linked to the lore and legend of what today we perceive and view as dragons, and some of these creatures are distinctly different to each other. But that should not take away from the fact that dragons are a real phenomenon."

On this latter point, Freeman elaborates:

> "I am absolutely certain, having reviewed many ancient reports of dragon activity, that many sightings – perhaps two or three hundred years ago and probably further back – were genuine encounters, but where the witnesses were seeing what I believe to have been huge snakes, giant crocodiles, and the Australian 'monster lizard' Megalania."

Freeman makes a noteworthy, and thought-provoking, point:

> "Any mention of dragons always conjures up images of fire-breathing monsters, and there are definitely reports that fall into that group. But, when you look into many of the earliest, ancient legends, you find that the dragon is more often associated with water. So, I have a theory that some of the better lake monster accounts from centuries ago may well have influenced dragon tales."

On this point, he adds:

> "Personally, I also believe that some classic tales of dragons in England in Medieval times, and tales of beasts such as the Lambton Worm, probably have their origins in lake monster accounts, giant eels, etc., that have then

mutated into tales of dragons on the loose. But the important point is that this shouldn't detract from the fact that people did see something."

I asked him: "You mean that the ancients were seeing lake monsters and, having been exposed to dragon legends, believed them to be – or interpreted them as - dragons, too?"

"Exactly," Freeman replied.

Of course, the biggest question of all was: are there creatures still living today that Freeman believes have helped perpetuate the image of the dragon? He is certain there are:

> "I would pretty much stake my life on the fact that Megalania still exists – or did until very recently – in the large forests of Australia, and that also roamed New Guinea. This was a huge, killer-beast; a massive monitor lizard that exceeded thirty feet in length. In literal terms, this was a classic dragon-type animal."

I questioned Freeman about his research into an animal known as the Naga of Thailand that he believes is responsible for some dragon tales. He told me:

> "There is no excuse for not getting out into the field and doing firsthand investigations; none at all. In fact, it's vital. I have no time for the armchair theorist. And one of the experiences that I will remember for the rest of my life was traveling to Thailand with the Discovery Channel in 2000, where we chased giant snakes – the Naga – in the caves and tunnels that exist deep below Thailand.
>
> "It's very easy to see why the inhabitants in times past considered them to be dragons. The Naga is apparently a large snake, a very large one – maybe in the order of literally tens of feet in length, oil-drum-sized bodies, and definitely big enough to take a whole man."

And similar accounts abound elsewhere, too:

> "There have come reports from the Congo of an animal known as Mokele-mbembe. Again, it has cross-over qualities with dragon legends, but I'm sure that it will be shown in time to be some sort of giant monitor lizard, too."

But what of the definitive, fire-breathing dragons of legend: does, or did, such a creature exist? Freeman makes a very intriguing observation:

> "Back in 1979 Peter Dickinson wrote a book that was titled *The Flight of Dragons*. Dickinson had come up with this idea – an excellent theory, in fact – that real-life dragons did exist and that they were the descendents of dinosaurs such as the Tyrannosaurus Rex. Dickinson suggested that these animals developed large, expanded stomachs that would fill with hydrogen gas,

which would come from a combination of hydrochloric acid found in the juices of the digestive system that would then mix with calcium found in the bones of their prey.

"Then, from there, the hydrogen – a lighter-than-air gas – allowed these creatures to take to the skies and then control their flight by burning off the excess gas in the form of flame. Anyone seeing this would be seeing the closest thing to the image of the dragon that we all know and love. Dickinson's theory is an excellent one, and may well be a perfect explanation for sightings of real dragons – in times past, and perhaps today, I believe."

And what does Freeman hope that his book, *Dragons: More Than a Myth?* will achieve? He says:

"Well, this is the first time that a trained zoologist, and a former head-keeper of reptiles at a major zoo, has written about dragons in a serious, scientific fashion and in a way that doesn't relegate the subject to just myths and tales. Something is going on and people are seeing something. I hope people will realize that I have tracked these animals – in all of their various guises and forms – and have presented the evidence in a way that I believe demonstrates that we do have some very strange beasts living among us."

Having read Freeman's fascinating work, I can only concur. I leave the final word to Freeman, the world's only professional dragon hunter:

"The dragon has its teeth and claws deep into the collective psyche of mankind, and its not about to let go. Our most ancient fear still stalks the earth today. Beware: this is no fairytale. When your parents told you that there were no such things as dragons, they lied!"

At the Edge 2006

From October 2005 to March 2006, Dana and I lived in the Texan city of Amarillo (and, yes, as it happens, I *do* know the way to Amarillo…); where, upon pulling up in town on our proud white stallions (okay, in our *Nissan Maxima*), I quickly sought out all the local media-outlets and offered them my services. One of those who said 'yes' to my offer of articles (actually the *only* one that said 'yes') was a local, weekly what's-on guide called *The Edge*. I penned a couple of items for the magazine during our brief time in town; the first of which was titled *Weird Texas*, and appeared in its pages in February 2006:

It's official: Texas is weird! Recently published by Sterling Publishing Co., is an excellent book titled *Weird Texas: Your Travel Guide to Texas's Local Legends and Best Kept Secrets*. Written by paranormal hunters Wesley Treat, Heather Shade, and Rob Riggs, this is a book that you are definitely going to want to read. In fact, it's one of those books best read by candlelight on a dark and stormy evening, or around a flickering campfire in the depths of the woods at midnight.

Covering practically every inch of the Lone Star State, *Weird Texas* contains chapters on ghosts, local legends, heroes and villains from Texan history, haunted houses, ancient mysteries, UFOs, strange animals, and much more, too.

The book is superbly put together, and its 280-plus pages are packed with full-color photographs, drawings, and renditions of the places, people, and creatures described within its pages. And, thank goodness, the book contains a lot of humor, adventure and intrigue that makes *Weird Texas* an absolute pleasure to read. Of course, some of the stories fall more into the realm of folklore than reality; but that doesn't mean that you won't get a big kick out of reading them.

As the book states:

> "With notepads and cameras in hand and steeds of one sort or another at the ready, Wesley Treat, Heather Shade, and Rob Riggs travelled the highways, byways, back roads, and all roads in between in search of the odd and offbeat. They tracked down impossible-to-believe tales only to discover an odd grain of truth that gives the stories just enough credibility to make one feel a little uncomfortable. Whether it's a goatman, a mystery airship, haunted cemeteries, or bouncing ghost lights, our authors have researched and chronicled the stories and presented them here, for you, fellow admirers of the weird."

And you will be intrigued to learn that Amarillo features within the packed pages of *Weird Texas*. Cadillac Ranch gets a good mention, as do the Ozymandias Legs. Like the buried Cadillacs, the gigantic Legs, which stand just off I-27, were the brainchild of a local man. And the story behind their construction is both amusing and informative.

While the entire book makes for fascinating reading, and demonstrates the sheer scale of high-strangeness that pervades much of Texas, it is the chapter titled "Bizarre Beasts" that I found most interesting. Written exclusively by Rob Riggs, this chapter reveals the incredible wealth of testimony and data in support of the notion that the forests of East Texas (that amount to an incredible sixteen million acres) are home to strange beasts, not unlike the alleged Bigfoot of the Pacific Northwest. Much of Rob's research has focused upon an area called the Big Thicket, from where countless tales and legends have surfaced of strange, hairy, shambling creatures, of wild men, of giant footprints embedded in the muddy banks of rivers, of weird lights in the sky, and much more of a bizarre and entertaining nature.

On the UFO angle, the book contains a large body of data on the famous Marfa Lights, the Ghost Lights of Bragg Road, and Texas's very own Roswell incident – the alleged crash of a UFO at the town of Aurora in 1897. Seen by many as just a hoax, the tale has nevertheless become embroiled in the collective weirdness of Texas. And for those of you interested in the paranormal, you can learn all about chain-rattling ghosts, spooky spectres, and Texas's most haunted towns and motels.

The good thing about this book is that it is one that you can read from beginning to end, or just pick up and delve into at random – and it will still entertain you. And if you are even remotely interested in the subjects described above, then you should take the opportunity to purchase a copy right now.

Having lived in Texas for the last 5 years, and having visited many of the places cited within the pages of the book, I can safely say that the team behind the book has done an excellent job of chronicling the genuine oddities (the paranormal, the amusing, and the downright strange) that can be found within Texas.

My second article for *The Edge* was titled *Strange Tales of the Lone Star State*:

Space Girl Dead on Spaghetti Junction

Since the publication of my review of a book titled *Weird Texas* that appeared in the February issue of this magazine, I have been contacted by a number of readers of *The Edge* asking if there are any other good books available on the mysteries of Texas. The answer to that question is yes, there most definitely are!

Certainly one of the most entertaining and informative is a book written by Austin-based author Lisa Farwell that is titled *Haunted Texas Vacations: The Complete Ghostly Guide*. From the *Bygone Boos of Jefferson* to the *Specters of San Antonio*, the small towns, big cities, and vast countryside of Texas offer prime ghost-hunting possibilities. Intended for those with a healthy and a lighthearted interest in all things supernatural, *Haunted Texas Vacations* tells you all that you need to know to plan a haunted vacation in the Lone Star State, and increase your chances of seeing something strange.

An engaging storyteller, author Lisa Farwell traveled to the spookiest and most historic locales in Texas – including much of the Panhandle – to research and write this compilation of more than 150 haunted places and their respective ghostly tales – presented along with practical information for organizing your trip, documenting your experiences, and sharing them with fellow ghost enthusiasts. Lisa holds a B.S. in advertising and is President of the *Capital City Ghost Research Society*. Also, she is an active member of the *American Ghost Research Society*. Check out her book. If you are a fan of tales of creepy haunted houses, you will not be disappointed.

Covering a somewhat similar path is Vallie Fletcher Taylor's *Spirits of Texas* that is packed with tales of the ghosts of ancient Indian tribes, spectral cattle-driving cowboys, murderers, and a host of other stories from the plains of the Panhandle to the forests of East Texas and the Rio Grande. With chapter titles like *Old Hico and a Ghost Named Henry*, *The Wedding Chapel Specter*, *The Phantom Chief*, and *Town Forgotten*, this is a great little book (it runs to 173 pages), and Taylor definitely knows how to write a good, atmospheric story and catch the reader's attention. Like Lisa Farwell, Taylor has the perfect background to write such a book: she is a member of the *Texas Folklore Society*, the *Austin Writers' League*, and the *International Women Writers' Guild*.

And if you are interested in the actions and adventures of weird animals, such as Bigfoot, Rob Riggs' *In the Big Thicket* is the perfect title to get your hands on at the earliest opportunity. *In the Big thicket* makes profound intrusions into what we call "reality." And there are allegedly some *very* weird things going on in this region of East Texas, including: "ghost lights;" spectral Indians; howling, ape-like "wild men;" and fireballs that streak through the nighttime skies – all of which defy both our common sense notions of space-time and all attempts at scientific explanation. So come along, if you dare, for a trek through the heart of this primeval forest. You'll emerge with a heightened sense of wonder and a deeper appreciation of the world of the unexplained.

Indeed, Rob Riggs' book even caused Dan Rather to comment that: "[Riggs'] thoroughness as a journalist and knowledge of the area show through on every page." And if Dan Rather was captivated by Riggs' book, then I think that this says a lot about the quality and credibility of the strange stories related therein. And Riggs is no gullible fool: he is a professional journalist and the former publisher of a series of award-winning community newspapers in Texas. His interest in "ghost lights," "wild man" sightings, and related phenomena began as a child when he heard tales about them in his hometown of Sour Lake in Big Thicket country. Riggs began writing about the subject more than twenty years ago while working as a reporter for the *Kountze News*. Since then his studies of unexplained phenomena have been featured in the *Houston Chronicle* and the *Beaumont Enterprise* newspapers.

And if UFOs are your cup of tea, then I definitely recommend that you read John Schuessler's *The Cash-Landrum UFO Incident*. The book tells the strange and disturbing story of two women and a young boy who, in December 1980, were driving late at night outside of Houston when they came across a brightly-lit UFO hovering over the road that was surrounded by a large group of military helicopters. Some researchers, the book demonstrates, thought that the UFO was really a secret, prototype military aircraft of some kind, while others consider it to have been truly out of this world in origin. Whatever the truth of this quarter-of-a-century old case, it *still* provokes interest and controversy to this day; and John Schuessler's book leaves no stone unturned in its quest for the truth.

And also on the subject of UFOs, there is David R. Wheeler's now-out-of-print book *The Lubbock Lights* that tells you all that you need to know about the history of *X-Files* style strangeness in the Panhandle.

The Tumbleweed - my main memory of West Texas.

Opening the Government's X-Archive 2006

I was still writing for the *Daily Express* newspaper in 2006, and still faithfully mining the paranormal and paranoid world of *The X-Files* – something that was, perhaps, most obvious in the following article I penned for the newspaper in that very same year, and to which I applied the highly-cheesy and predictable title of *Opening the Government's X-Archive*. Hell, I had something like 7-hours notice that the editor wanted the article; and so, with Fleet Street waiting, there was no time at all for fancy and original titles. I cracked open a cold one or two, cranked up *The Freshies* on the CD-player, and pounded it out. And here it is:

Previously-secret Government documents show that the adventures of everyone's favourite paranormal investigators, FBI agents Mulder and Scully, may be closer to the truth than we think.

UFOs and the Condign Report

Some believe that the British Government is hiding evidence that UFOs exist. Others view this belief as paranoia and delusion. The controversy intensified when, in May of this year, it was announced that after decades of secretly investigating UFOs, the Ministry of Defence had come to the conclusion that aliens were not visiting Britain. The MoD's claims were revealed within the pages of a formerly classified *X-Files*-style document that had been commissioned in 1996 and that was completed in February 2000.

Obtained under the terms of the Freedom of Information Act (FOIA) by Dr. David Clarke of

Sheffield University, and titled the Condign Report, the 465-page document demonstrated how air defence experts had decided that UFO sightings were probably the result of 'natural, but relatively rare phenomena' such as ball-lightning and atmospheric plasmas. UFOs, wrote the still-unknown author of the MoD's report, were 'of no defence significance'.

Inevitably, UFO investigators claimed that the MoD's report was merely a ruse to hide its secret knowledge of aliens. And although the Government denied such claims, the Condign Report did reveal a number of significant conclusions.

The atmospheric plasmas which were believed to be the cause of so many UFO reports were 'still barely understood', said the MoD; and the magnetic and electric fields that emanated from plasmas could adversely affect the human nervous system. Significantly, the MoD also concluded that Russia and the United States were probably researching those same plasmas to determine if they could be used as a weapon of war.

A Close Encounter of the Hairy Kind

The hope and assumption of many is that if aliens are visiting us, they mean us no harm. But that may not be the case. Classified for decades and now available to the public is a three-page Royal Air Force document that relates the disturbing facts of a UFO encounter reported to the RAF in 1966 by a young lady named Diane Foulkes.

She had been driving towards her Shrewsbury home late on the night of 8 November 1966 when, according to the RAF's archives, a circular-shaped UFO loomed into view as she neared the River Severn.

Corporal R.A. Rickwood of the RAF's Provost and Security Services wrote in his report:

> '...she could see rays of light shooting from the object which appeared to keep station with her car until she arrived home. At one time during the journey the object travelled near her and the rays seemed to come towards the right hand side of her car. She felt a bump against that side as if they had struck it.'

Corporal Rickwood continued:

> 'At this moment she felt as if she had received an electric shock and had felt a severe pain in her neck. The left-hand side headlight of the car also went out. This made her extremely frightened. When she got home she felt very ill and had complained to her parents.'

After completing his investigation, Corporal Rickwood came to a conclusion:

> 'There is no evidence to associate the incidents complained of with the Royal Air Force and the complainant Miss Foulkes is now satisfied that the incidents are unexplainable and in no way connected with the Armed

Forces.'

And, as a result, the investigation of this strange case was quietly closed.

Big Cats on the Prowl

For decades, people have reported seeing so-called 'big cats' prowling around the British countryside. Many are in no doubt that the creatures exist, and some suspect them to be zoo escapees.

In a statement made in the House of Commons in 1998, however, then-Parliamentary Secretary to the Ministry of Agriculture, Fisheries and Food, Elliot Morley, confidently assured the House that: 'Until we obtain stronger evidence, the reports of big cats are still in the category of mythical creatures.'

Thanks to the FOIA, we now have that 'stronger evidence'.

Replying earlier this year to a FOIA request from a member of the public with an interest in big cat sightings seen in Hampshire between 1995 and 2005, the county's Police Force released files that stated:

> 'Hampshire's Constabulary's Air Support Unit has been deployed to assist with the following reports: January 1995 – Black Panther like animal seen in Eastleigh. Two likely heat sources found by the aircraft, but nothing found by ground troops. March 1995 – Black Puma like animal seen in Winchester. One heat source found that could not be classified by the aircraft crew, kept running off from searching officers, search eventually abandoned.'

Notably, when a similar FOIA request was filed with Sussex Police in late 2005, documentation was made available to the requester that read as follows:

> 'Firearms officers have been deployed in response to such a report on one occasion, on 22 July 2004 – sighting by a member of the public in Seaford. The area was searched, but no trace was found of such an animal.'

The story is far more spectacular on the east coast, however. In 1991, documents show, a lynx – that the Department for Environment, Food and Rural Affairs believed may have escaped from a zoo – was shot dead near Great Witchingham, Norfolk, by a man who then placed the body in his freezer before selling it to a local collector who had the creature stuffed.

It transpires that an extensive dossier on the affair was opened by local police that – as with the above-reports on other exotic felines prowling the British countryside – would have remained under lock and key were it not for the FOIA.

It all began when police officers were investigating a gamekeeper who, it was suspected, was responsible for the deaths of a number of birds of prey in the area. The officer that interviewed the man in question wrote in his now-declassified report:

> 'At the start of the search in an outhouse, which contained a large chest freezer, I asked him what he had in the freezer, and he replied: "Oh, only some pigeons and a lynx." On opening the freezer there was a large lynx lying stretched out in the freezer on top of a load of pigeons! He had shot this when he saw it chasing his gun dog.'

Britain's big cats, it seems, are no longer a myth.

The Real X-File

It is often claimed – and accepted by many – that UFOs are never seen by trained observers, such as military personnel. The FOIA, however, has shown this to be far from true. A perfect case in point is a series of spectacular UFO encounters that occurred over the British Isles on 31 March 1993. Records reveal that the Ministry of Defence took the incidents very seriously.

One of the most intriguing encounters, the documentation reveals, came from a man who had seen, at shortly after 1.00 a.m., an object 'oval' in shape, 'approximately 150 metres in length', and that made a 'loud humming noise' as it flew over the Cannock Chase forest, and near the Staffordshire town of Brereton.

From there, Ministry of Defence files demonstrate, at around 1.15 a.m., the object flew over RAF Cosford, near Wolverhampton, and was witnessed by staff working at the base. According to a report filed by one of the base personnel:

> 'I was on mobile patrol when I saw two bright lights in the sky above the Airfield. The lights appeared to be flying at great velocity. The lights were circular in shape and gave off no beam. They were creamy white in colour. A slight red glow could be seen from the rear of the lights as they disappeared from view.'

Shortly afterwards, records show, the meteorological officer at RAF Shawbury saw something that left him baffled too, as the following extract from the MoD's dossier makes clear:

> 'The lights were first sighted approximately 15-20 kms away and Mr. [Deleted] observed them travel towards him over the Airfield moving erratically at hundreds of miles per hour unlike any aircraft. He described the lights as appearing to be searching for something. He heard a low humming noise and watched the objects for 5 minutes until it disappeared from sight.'

And although UFO authority Dr. David Clarke believes that the bulk of the reports may have been caused by space debris burning-up in the earth's atmosphere, within the Ministry of Defence, the case remains unexplained to this day.

The Monster Files

Some of us may think that a still-living dinosaur lurks within the deep waters of Loch Ness. Others may believe that the stories are nothing more than a ploy to help boost Scotland's economy. For Whitehall civil servants, however, the nation's most famous monster – Nessie – has secretly been a favourite topic of investigation for decades.

In the late 1970s, documents made available to the public in 2005 reveal, the then-Conservative government of Margaret Thatcher had seriously considered a request to use dolphins in a search for Nessie. If the existence of the monster could be proven, Whitehall thought, it would have a very positive bearing upon Scotland's tourist industry. Amid complaints from the Scottish Society for the Prevention of Cruelty to Animals, however, the plan was never put into action. But still the Nessie file remained open.

In the mid-1980s, Whitehall civil servants were tasked with determining if the Loch Ness Monster was at risk from hunters and poachers. At one point, government officials were seriously considering drafting new legislation to protect Nessie – a creature that no one could be sure even existed.

Eventually, FOIA-declassified documents show, the government concluded that: 'The legislative framework to protect the monster is available; provided she (or he) is identified by scientists whose reputation will carry weight with the British Museum.'

Of course, so far no such identification has been made. Unless someone in Whitehall knows something we don't. And perhaps they do. In 1965, additional files show, the Royal Air Force's Joint Air Reconnaissance Intelligence Centre at RAF Brampton analysed film footage taken in 1960 that purported to show the Loch Ness Monster and concluded:

> 'One can presumably rule out the idea that it is any sort of submarine vessel for various reasons which leaves the conclusion that it is probably an animate object.'

The Dowsing Detective

During the Second World War, Warwickshire Police Force secretly used one of its own officers skilled in the art of dowsing to try and locate the bodies of two local men – James Hiatt and Harry Marston - that had been buried under the rubble caused by the bombs of Nazi Germany.

We assume that dowsing is something specifically employed to locate underground bodies of water – not secret searches for dead bodies. Our assumption may be wrong.

A once-classified report of July 1941 that was prepared by a Sergeant J. Hall states:

> 'I was at the scene when I noticed P.C. 319 Terry coming from a nearby thicket fashioning a forked stick with a pen-knife. P.C. Terry commenced to walk over the bomb craters. About 30 seconds later he came to a standstill

and I noticed that the forked stick which he was holding had commenced to wriggle very violently and he had great difficulty in holding it. He pointed to a particular portion of heaped soil near to one of the craters and said: "They are under there."'

Sergeant Hall added:

'A quarter of an hour later the bodies of both men were recovered.'

Notably, the files reveal, the government's Ministry of Home Security expressed scepticism over the whole affair, and concluded that the Warwickshire Police Force's use of 'spiritualism' and 'the mysterious' in such a fashion during wartime was 'particularly dangerous'.

Crop Circles

While many people are of the opinion that Crop Circles are the work of hoaxers, on at least one occasion government personnel expressed great concern about this most familiar mystery of the modern age. At the height of the Second World War, documentation that has surfaced

Crop Watching.

from MI5 shows, the Government had become aware of circular formations of flattened corn, 'twenty metres in diameter', that had been found in fields across war-torn Europe.

British Intelligence worried that the formations were messages left for Nazi bomber pilots. Files demonstrate, however, that this was never ultimately proven to be the case.

Two decades later, in 1964, the MoD received the report of a man who had found an 'almost perfect circle' on land near Penrith, Cumbria. Despite the fact that the man had seen a strange 'column of blue light about eight feet in diameter' that seemed to be associated with the circular formation, on this occasion the Government was less concerned than during wartime. MoD investigators merely dismissed the case amid in-house speculation about the condition of the witness's liver.

Is The Truth Really Out There?

Is the fact that government agencies secretly investigate strange phenomena of the types described above an indication that those same phenomena really exist? Or is it simply the case that the official world is obliged to investigate anything and everything – no matter how weird - that is brought to its attention, regardless of how credible it considers the information to be? As more and more documents from the real *X-Files* of the Government surface via the FOIA, we may one day learn the answers to those questions. The truth may be out there, after all.

The Strange Saga of the Hexham Heads 2006

Tales of werewolves and lycanthropy have intrigued and fascinated me for just about as long as I can remember; and the menacing legend of Northumberland's Hexham Heads truly takes some beating when it comes to the high-strangeness-stakes. So, when *Fate* editor Phyllis Galde asked me, in 2006, if I could prepare an article on that very subject for her, I was pleased to oblige. And here's the result, *The Strange Saga of the Hexham Heads*:

On December 10, 1904, a startling story appeared in the pages of the English newspaper, the *Hexham Courant*. Under the heading of *Wolf at Large in Allendale*, it read: "Local farmers from the village of Allendale, very near to Hexham, had reported the loss of their livestock, so serious that many sheep were being stabled at night to protect them. A shepherd found two of his flock slaughtered, one with its entrails hanging out, and all that remained of the other was its head and horns. Many of the sheep had been bitten about the neck and the legs – common with an attack made by a wolf."

The newspaper article continued: "Hysteria soon set in. During the night, lanterns were kept burning to scare away the wolf, and women and children were ordered to keep to the busy roads and be home before dusk. The 'Hexham Wolf Committee' was soon set up to organize search parties and hunts to bring down the beast using specialized hunting dogs, the 'Haydon Hounds', but even they could not find the wolf. The Wolf Committee took the next step and hired Mr. W. Briddick, a trained tracker. But he was also unsuccessful, despite searching the woods."

On January 7, 1905, however, there was a major development: the *Hexham Courant* reported that the body of a wolf had been found dead on a railway track at Cumwinton, Cumbria – which was approximately thirty miles from where the majority of the attacks had been occurring. However, it was the newspaper's firm opinion that this was not the same creature, but yet another one. In other words, the mystery beast of Hexham was still out there.

Indeed, according to some theorists, there was a whole pack of such animals wildly roaming the countryside of northern England by night. And although the searches for the animal, or animals, continued for some time, they were finally brought to a halt when the attacks abruptly stopped. Hexham's mysterious and wolfish visitor had gone.

In 1972, however, it may well have returned – albeit in a slightly different guise.

And as evidence of this, we have to turn our attention to the bizarre story of the Hexham Heads.

The strange saga all began in February 1972. An eleven-year-old boy and his younger brother, whose family name was Robson, were digging up weeds in their parents' back garden in the town of Hexham, when they unearthed two carved, stone heads, slightly smaller than a tennis ball and very heavy in weight. Crudely fashioned and weathered-looking, one resembled a skull-like masculine head crowned by a Celtic hairstyle; while the other was a slightly smaller female head that possessed what were said to be witch-like qualities, including the classic beaked nose.

Shortly after the boys had taken the heads into their house, a number of peculiar incidents occurred in the family home. The heads would move by themselves. Household objects were found inexplicably broken. And at one point the boys' sister found her bed showered with glass. However, it was the next-door neighbours who would experience the most bizarre phenomena of all.

A few nights after the discovery of the heads, a mother living in the neighbouring house, Ellen Dodd, was sitting up late with her daughter, who was suffering with toothache, when both saw what they described as a hellish, "half-man, half-beast" enter the room. Naturally, both screamed for their lives and the woman's husband came running from another room to see what all the commotion was about.

By this stage, however, the hairy creature had fled the room and could be heard "padding down the stairs as if on its hind legs." The front door was later found wide open and it was presumed that the creature had left the house in haste.

Soon after the incident, one Anne Ross – a doctor who had studied the Celtic culture and who was the author of several books on the subject, including *Pagan Celtic Britain* and *The Folklore of the Scottish Highlands* – took possession of the stone heads to study them herself. She already had in her possession several similar heads and was certain that the Hexham Heads were Celtic in origin and probably nearly two thousand years old. The doctor, who lived in the

English city of Southampton and about 150 miles from Hexham, had heard nothing at that time of the strange goings-on encountered by the previous owners of the heads.

Having put the two stone heads with the rest of her collection, however, Dr. Ross, too, encountered the mysterious werewolf-like creature a few nights later. She awoke from her sleep feeling cold and frightened and, on looking up found herself confronted by a horrific man-beast identical to that seen at Hexham.

"It was about six feet high," Dr. Ross recalled,

> "slightly stooping, and it was black, against the white door, and it was half animal and half man. The upper part, I would have said, was a wolf, and the lower part was human and, I would have again said, that it was covered with a kind of black, very dark fur. It went out and I just saw it clearly, and then it disappeared, and something made me run after it, a thing I wouldn't normally have done, but I felt compelled to run after it. I got out of bed and I ran, and I could hear it going down the stairs, then it disappeared toward the back of the house."

After this startling and terrifying event, the doctor and her family saw on several subsequent occasions what they described as a huge black creature, not unlike the classic description of a werewolf materialize within the confines of the house. It invariably appeared on the stairs, said the doctor, and would then jump over the banisters to land in the hall, whereupon it would exit at high speed on what sounded like padded feet. And at other times, the beast could be heard padding around unseen, while doors would fly open seemingly for no reason at all.

On another occasion, Dr. Ross and her husband, the archaeologist (and author of the books *A Guide to Prehistoric Scotland* and *From Windmill Hill to Hadrian's Wall*) Richard Feachem

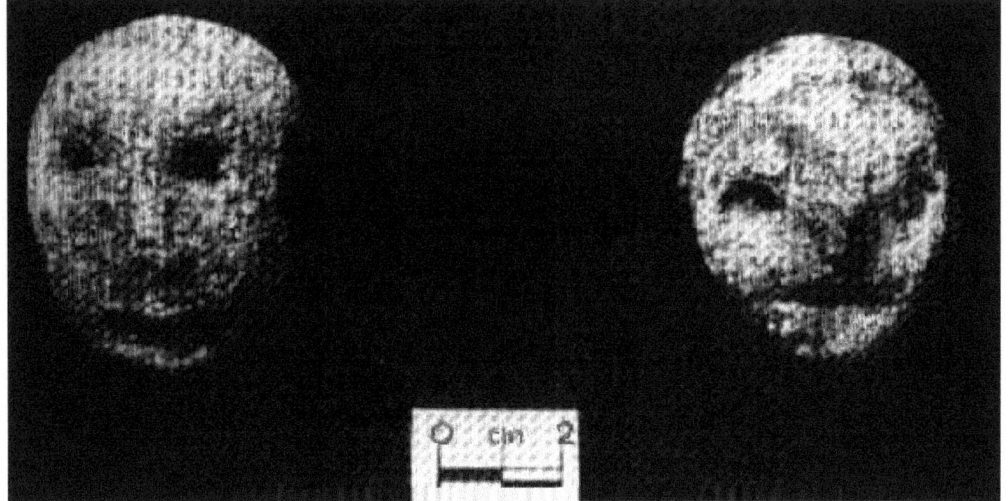

returned home one evening after a visit to London to find their daughter, Berenice, in a state of considerable distress after she, too, encountered the mystery animal.

According to Dr. Ross, there was "an evil presence about the house" and she eventually decided that the stone heads were the source of the problem and promptly got rid of the entire collection. At some point afterwards, the heads are known to have been displayed at the British Museum; but were reportedly withdrawn amid rumors of "eerie events" allegedly having occurred in their presence.

The Hexham Heads also reached the hands of Don Robins – author of *Circles of Silence*, and a player in British author Paul Devereux's *Dragon Project*; the purpose of which was to study claims that certain British prehistoric sites had unusual forces or energies attached to them, including magnetic, infrared and ultrasonic anomalies.

Notably, while investigating one such site – the megalithic Rollright Stones which can be found near the English village of Long Compton, and which border the counties of Oxfordshire and Warwickshire – Paul Devereux reported that one of the team members (described as being a "well-known archaeologist") was sitting in a van when "a very large, hairy animal walked by. He said it had coarse, gray hair and it went by. He wondered: 'What could that be?' And he looked out and there was nothing there."

Don Robins subsequently provided the Hexham Heads to a dowser named Frank Hyde, who tried to determine if they possessed paranormal qualities, and who apparently utilized copper mesh in an attempt to lessen their strange effects – something that was reportedly successful.

The two Hexham Heads then fell into the hands of other collectors, none of whom experienced any werewolf-like encounters in the dead of night. Some, however, did report that the sense of pure evil, which seemed to specifically emit from the witchlike head, made them feel extremely uncomfortable.

Interestingly, the previous owner of the house in Hexham, where the heads were discovered, claimed later that he had, in fact, carved the heads as toys for his children in the 1950s and that they had been lost in the yard years before. Yet, this claim is disputed by many that have delved into the puzzle. And although tests were undertaken at both Southampton University and Newcastle University to try and confirm the real ages of the heads, the results of those tests remain tantalizingly unknown, and they were eventually lost.

The current whereabouts of the Hexham Heads remains mysteriously – and perhaps appropriately - unknown.

Happy Anniversary, Roswell UFO 2007

Ah yes, Roswell: where would Ufology be without its cosmic (or not) Holy-Grail? Roswell is, of course, the one case that, for many, keeps the extra-terrestrial-hypothesis alive and kicking. For me, today, Roswell is nothing more than an *X-Files* version of Jack the Ripper: namely, an ancient case, an event filled to the brim with a variety of theories, one that will never be resolved to the satisfaction of everyone, but also one for which whole swathes of the UFO research community must continue to fly the flag. Belief and faith are very strong things. And, in the town of Roswell itself, the legendary crash (of aliens, of Japanese prisoners-of-war, or of crash-test-dummies – depending on who you ask and whose version of events you believe) has spawned a veritable industry. So, when the 60th anniversary of the now-utterly-deathly-boring affair lumbered around in July 2007, the *Daily Express* invited me to submit an article on the matter for their readers – which I duly did. It went like this:

With the 60th anniversary of the infamous UFO crash at Roswell, New Mexico looming on the horizon, paranormal author Nick Redfern takes a trip back in time to the controversial incident, and looks closely at the dramatic effect that the strange events of early July 1947 had on the people of Roswell, the town itself, and its thriving, UFO-driven economy.

Situated in south-eastern New Mexico, the town of Roswell, with a bustling population of just under 50,000 people, is today the state's fifth largest city. It has a thriving farming industry, it is a major producer of the nation's petroleum, and was the birth place of both Hollywood actress Demi Moore and the late country-and-western singer, John Denver. And, all thanks to a controversial (and, some say, out-of-this-world) incident that occurred sixty years ago, Roswell is today one of the leading tourist attractions in the United States.

Every year, countless UFO believers, *X-Files* fans and holiday-makers flock to Roswell hoping to learn if aliens from across the galaxy really did crash to earth on a fateful day back in early July 1947. The American Government and the Air Force firmly say no. Conspiracy theorists and UFO researchers enthusiastically say yes. And, as a result, widespread publicity inevitably abounds. All of which, of course, makes the people of Roswell very happy.

Indeed, in much the same way that the Loch Ness Monster generates a sizeable and welcome income for the Scottish Tourist Board, so Roswell owes a significant amount of its own revenue to the legendary little green men that are said to have fallen to their deaths in the desert all those years ago.

Even the briefest of strolls along the bustling North Main Street that runs through the centre of Roswell makes for a truly surreal experience: the outside of the local McDonald's restaurant is shaped like a classic flying saucer. Mums and Dads can treat their kids to meals of ET burgers and chips. Posters of UFOs and Flying Saucers adorn the shops. The town's lamp-posts are topped off with alien heads, complete with huge black-eyes. And when you get thirsty, why not pay a visit to the Alien Caffeine Espresso Bar?

Then there is the International UFO Museum. Opened to the public in 1992, it has attracted more than a million visitors in the past fifteen years, and boasts displays of dead alien bodies laid out on tables, models and pictures of the alleged crashed UFO and its crew, as well as numerous displays devoted to Crop Circles, the infamous Area 51, and alien abductions. And visitors to the museum have plenty to spend their money on, too, including 'alien Christmas stockings', 'Roswell Coffee', Christmas Tree decorations adorned with UFO imagery, and, for dog-lovers, even t-shirts for your favourite pooch that celebrate the famous 1947 incident.

Yes: Roswell and space-aliens go together like, well, Mulder and Scully.

To celebrate their status as a true Mecca for alien investigators, as well as those who just want to know what all of the fuss is really about, every year the people of Roswell hold a weekend-long UFO festival to commemorate the day that forever changed their otherwise unremarkable town. And, as the first weekend in July of this year marks the 60th anniversary of the Roswell crash, the festival organisers are preparing to be overwhelmed by thousands of people, each and everyone eager to learn the latest news, views and revelations on the alien top secrets of Roswell.

In addition to lectures from best-selling British and American UFO authors, the festival also boasts appearances by rock-singer Alan Parsons; actor and comedian Dean Haglund, who had a recurring role on *The X-Files*; and Chase Masterson, co-star of television's *Star Trek: Deep Space Nine* series, who was recently voted one of the 'fifty sexiest women of the year' by *Femme Fatales Magazine*. And then there is the not-to-be-missed 'alien golf' tournament. In other words, a good time should be had by one and all.

And what do the locals think of their town's out-of-this world reputation? Roswell mayor, Bill B. Owen, says: 'I checked my birth certificate and it says 1953, so I wasn't around in 1947, so I don't know what happened. On the serious side, I think if you listen to all the evidence that you have to have a question in your mind that something unusual happened. It is a mystery that is not likely to be solved.'

Local man Bill Shaw says:

> 'I've seen Roswell go from a small town to like something out of *Star Trek*. But we're a friendly town; and the UFO story brings people in. Whatever it was that crashed, Roswell has a lot to be thankful for. It's put the town on the map. Every July, when the UFO people arrive, it just gets crazy.'

Indeed, this is echoed by Roswell's official website that states: 'Roswell has something to offer all of our special visitors, whether from this planet, or a distant galaxy.'

But, needless to say, the town of Roswell hasn't always been quite so unusual. In 1869, Van C. Smith, a Nebraskan businessman, and his partner Aaron Wilburn visited what was then an utterly desolate area and constructed two buildings: namely a grocery shop and a post-office. Two years later, having secured ownership of the land from the government, Smith named the dusty, desert location after his father: Roswell Smith, a prominent Indiana-based lawyer. Van C. Smith then began to develop the land on a large scale, and thus was well and truly born a sleepy little New Mexican town called Roswell.

Even before the alleged UFO crash of 1947 supposedly occurred, however, Roswell had two brief claims to fame: First, it was where, in the 1930s, early rocket-pioneer Robert Goddard carried out his experiments; and, second, the Roswell Army Air Field base was home to the 509th Bomb Group that dropped the atomic bombs on the Japanese cities of Hiroshima and Nagasaki that brought the Second World War to a shuddering end. But even the devastating power of the atom cannot compete with UFOs, and has been completely eclipsed by all-things alien.

And even though, today, the strange events of early July 1947 are, for the most part, merely a source of fun and entertainment for those that want to spend a day in town, the fact remains that the incident that firmly put Roswell on the map so long ago, and gave it its place in the history books, is one that is still shrouded in deep mystery and intrigue.

No-one, not even the US Government in fact, disputes that *something* crashed to earth in the blistering hot and barren deserts of New Mexico in the summer of 1947. The event has been the subject of numerous books, official investigations undertaken by the U.S. Air Force, countless television documentaries, a hit movie starring actor Martin Sheen, and has left in its wake a legacy of controversy and a web of intrigue that continue to reverberate and rumble sixty years later.

It is a matter of record that in early July 1947, the then Army Air Forces announced to the entire world that they had recovered the broken remains of a 'flying disc' that had been found on a farm near Roswell by a rancher named William 'Mack' Brazel.

The intense media interest and speculation that followed for twenty-four hours was only brought to a close when the military hastily retracted that sensational statement: the flying disc story was a huge mistake and the wreckage originated with nothing stranger than a weather-balloon. Why trained military personnel from Roswell's elite 509th Bomb Group could not tell the difference between a flying saucer and a weather-balloon was never explained.

Today, the Air Force tells a *third* story: that the debris found at Roswell came not from a UFO nor from a weather-balloon, but from a top-secret balloon project – called 'Mogul' – that was designed to monitor the atmosphere for evidence of early Soviet atomic bomb tests.

But what about the small, mangled alien bodies that some people claim to have seen at the crash site? In a 1994 report, the military's official word was that the stories of extra-terrestrial corpses having been found in the New Mexico desert, and whisked away in secret were all complete nonsense. Three years later, the Air Force decided to modify its position.

In July 1997 – as everyone in the town of Roswell was busily gearing up for the fiftieth anniversary celebrations - the Pentagon revealed that, yes, bodies *were* found, after all; however, they were simply 'crash-test-dummies' used in high-altitude balloon experiments. The media bought the story. That is, until an astute journalist pointed out to the Government that its own records showed that the experiments with dummies did not even begin until early 1953, and more than five years after Roswell. Little wonder, therefore, that the Roswell saga continues to provoke both deep interest and cries of 'cover-up' a full six decades later. But UFOs, weather balloons, and crash-test-dummies are not the only theories that have been put forward in an attempt to lay the mystery of Roswell to rest once and for all.

According to some researchers, a captured German wartime V-2 rocket – with a small monkey aboard – was the cause of the legend. Others suggest - given the fact that Roswell was home to the 509th Bomb Group that turned Nagasaki and Hiroshima into radioactive wastelands in 1945 - some sort of atomic accident happened.

A far darker story – and one that is told in my own book on the case, *Body Snatchers in the Desert* - addresses claims that in 1947 New Mexico the U.S. Government was secretly engaged in several balloon-based, high-altitude-exposure experiments using human guinea-pigs, and that a number of such experiments failed; something which subsequently led the Air Force to bury the truth behind a mass of confusing and conflicting stories about dead aliens, crash-test-dummies, and weather balloons.

When I last visited the town of Roswell in December 2005, I asked one particular question of a number of Roswell residents: what would happen if Roswell was solved tomorrow and it was proven that aliens *didn't* crash to earth in 1947? The replies were intriguing, to say the least: 'No-one believes anything the government has said so far, so why should we believe their next story?' replied a postman who I stopped as he delivered the mail to the good folk of

Roswell.

'It doesn't matter; people will still keep believing,' said another. But certainly the most notable and telling statement was that of the shop-owner who derived a sizeable income from the sale of alien toys, novelty gifts, t-shirts, and videos: 'I don't even want to *think* about a question like that,' was his only, and tight-lipped, reply. Perhaps aliens really did crash at Roswell, New Mexico sixty years ago. On the other hand, maybe the U.S. Air Force is correct and nothing stranger than a balloon and crash-test-dummies fell to earth in 1947. Or could there be yet another explanation that currently remains buried deep within a batch of secret files that sit on a dusty shelf in a secure government archive? No-one really knows. But that is the point.

It is not so much the answers that attract people to Roswell. Rather, it is the fact that like an American version of Britain's Jack the Ripper, or the aforementioned Loch Ness Monster, Roswell continues to remain a mystery – and people, of course, love mysteries. And the fact that this particular mystery is shrouded in claims of high-level cover-up and conspiracy, as well as a multitude of conflicting and ever-changing explanations from the U.S. Government, only heightens the interest.

If the full story behind the admittedly still-intriguing Roswell affair is one day ultimately resolved, then UFO fans may be proven right, after all. On the other hand, if nothing stranger than the remains of a secret, military balloon were the cause of the so many tales that are part and parcel of the Roswell legend, then just like that same balloon, Roswell's tourist industry may burst in truly spectacular fashion.

Celebrating a Rendlesham Anniversary at the old military base.

Weirdness in the Woods 2007

That was the title of an article I wrote for *Beyond Magazine* in 2007, and which was focused upon that distinctly spooky area of woodland: Rendlesham Forest, Suffolk. Everyone's heard of the notorious 'UFO landing' at the nearby airbase in December 1980, right? It's a wild and strange story, indeed; one most graphically related within the packed-pages of *Left at East Gate*, written by Larry Warren and Peter Robbins. But, who knew that the forest was home to an absolute plethora of *additional* mysteries, too – including big-cats, hairy man-beasts, spooks, spectres and more? Yep: Rendlesham is officially weird. And here's the evidence, in the form of my article for the now-sadly-defunct *Beyond*:

Any mention of the mysterious locale that is Rendlesham Forest, Suffolk, England inevitably conjures up strange and surreal images of the famous UFO landing within the forest in the latter part of December 1980 – a startling event witnessed by numerous United States Air Force personnel stationed at a nearby military base: Royal Air Force Bentwaters. The bizarre affair has been the subject of a considerable number of books, numerous televisions shows, several investigations by military and governmental bodies, and unrelenting debate.

Reports of strange lights, of small alien-like creatures seen deep within the heart of the woods, and of high-level cover-ups and sinister conspiracies, are all key ingredients of the case that has justifiably become known as the 'British Roswell'.

Three decades on, the events in question continue to provoke intense debate and controversy; with some believing that extra-terrestrials really did land on British soil on that fateful night. Others hold the view that everything can be attributed to mistaken identity (of a lighthouse, no less!); while some prefer the theory that a dark and dubious military experiment, and subsequent mishap, may have been to blame for all of the fuss. Nearly thirty years on, the debate continues to rage; and doubtless it will continue to rage for many more years to come.

Rendlesham Forest covers an area that is around 1,500 hectares in size and can be found in Suffolk's coastal belt known as the Sandlings. It is comprised of large, coniferous trees, as well as heath land and wet land areas; and is home to the badger, the fox, the red deer, the roe deer and the fallow deer. According to some people, however, Rendlesham Forest is home to far stranger things, too…

In his authoritative book *Explore Phantom Black Dogs*, Bob Trubshaw recorded that: 'The folklore of phantom black dogs is known throughout the British Isles. From the Black Shuck of East Anglia to the Mauthe Dhoog of the Isle of Man there are tales of huge spectral hounds "darker than the night sky" with eyes "glowing red as burning coals". The phantom black dog of British and Irish folklore, which often forewarns of death, is part of a world-wide belief that dogs are sensitive to spirits and the approach of death, and keep watch over the dead and dying. North European and Scandinavian myths dating back to the Iron Age depict dogs as corpse eaters and the guardians of the roads to hell. Medieval folklore includes a variety of "Devil dogs" and spectral hounds.'

Although the image that the phantom black dog creates is one of a deadly and devilish beast that prowled the villages and towns of old England centuries ago, it is a little known fact outside of students of the phenomenon that occasional sightings of such creatures continue to surface to this very day; and from deep within Rendlesham Forest, no less.

On a cold winter's afternoon in 1983, for example, the soon-to-be-married Paul and Jane Jennings were blissfully strolling through the woods of Rendlesham when they were terrified by the sudden manifestation in front of them of what Jane would describe succinctly as 'a big black dog'. She elaborated that the pair had been walking along a pathway when, on rounding a bend, they came face to face with the phantom beast – something that prompted Jane to intriguingly add: 'It was almost like it was waiting for us.'

Reportedly, the beast's head was clearly canine in appearance, albeit much larger than that of any normal dog. Yet, somewhat curiously, its body seemed to exhibit characteristics that were distinctly feline-like in nature. For a brief and tense moment girlfriend and boyfriend stared at the creature, which, they recalled, seemed to have an eerily mournful expression upon its face.

Far more shocking, however, was what happened next. Suddenly, the beast began to 'flicker on and off for four or five times', then finally vanished, literally, before the Jennings' eyes amid an overwhelming smell that reminded the pair of 'burning metal'. Or, perhaps, brimstone would be a far better and more apt description. Not surprisingly, the terrified couple fled for the safety of their car and quickly left the area.

Rendlesham Forest, as well as the Suffolk locales of West Wratting and Balsham, is reportedly home to an even more diabolical beast than the phantom black dog. It is a creature that has come to be known locally as the Shug-Monkey. Described as being a bizarre combination of giant dog and large ape, the creature is said to strike deep terror into the hearts of those souls unfortunate enough to cross its path – which is something that Sam Holland can most definitely attest to.

Shortly after New Year's Day in 1956, Holland was walking through the woods with his spaniel dog, Harry, when he was horrified to see a bizarre-looking creature come looming out of the trees some forty feet in front of him. It walked upon four huge, muscular legs – 'like a lion's' – and its thick fur coat was both black and glossy. Incredibly, said Holland, the animal was easily ten feet in length; and so could not be considered anything even remotely resembling a domestic animal, or a known wild beast of the British Isles.

Holland recalled thinking for a moment that perhaps the animal was an exotic big cat that had escaped from a zoo or private estate; that is until it turned in his direction and he was finally able to see its terrible face. Likening it to that of a sliver-back gorilla, Holland said that the monstrous creature possessed a huge neck, widely flaring nostrils, and immense, powerful-looking jaws. For a moment or two, the animal looked intently at Holland and his whimpering little dog; then, seemingly losing interest, continued on its way and into the depths of the surrounding undergrowth. Holland would later explain that the creature looked like a strange combination of ape, dog, lion and rhinoceros.

Needless to say, the British Isles are not home to any such animal that even remotely resembles the beast that Sam Holland says he stumbled upon. Yet he is adamant that his description of the monstrous entity and his recollections of the day in question are utterly accurate. Today, Holland believes that whatever it was that he had the misfortune to run into half a century ago, it was unquestionably paranormal rather than physical in origin. But from where, precisely, he has no idea.

Rendlesham has also been the site of several intriguing encounters with what have become known as 'Alien Big Cats'- or ABCs. The infamous beasts of Bodmin and Exmoor are perhaps more well-known than their Suffolk-based cousins; however, the reports that have surfaced from in and around Rendlesham Forest are certainly no less provocative in nature.

One of the earliest, credible cases on record is that of Jimmy Freeman, whose close encounter with a big cat occurred while driving past Rendlesham Forest late one night in the mid-1970s. While the precise date has been lost to the inevitable fog of time (he feels that it was January of 1976, whereas his wife thinks that the event may have occurred twelve months later: in January of 1977), the details are as fresh in the mind of Freeman today as they were on the night the incident occurred.

Given the fact that the encounter had occurred around 11.15 to 11.30 on what was a dark, cloudy and slightly misty night, Freeman was driving slowly and had his lights on full-beam as he negotiated the dark and winding roads. As a result, when something large and shadowy charged across the road in front of him, Freeman could not fail to see the creature for what it was. Long, sleek and utterly black in colour, Freeman is in no doubt that for a split second or two he had a brief sighting of a huge cat. Today, he says firmly: 'If I live to be a hundred, I will tell the same: Rendlesham Forest has big cats.'

On an eerily similar path, in October 2003, it was reported that a woman named June Fooks, of Eyck, near Woodbridge – which is on the doorstep of Rendlesham Forest – had seen 'a black feline' in her garden that was 'bigger than her pet Labrador'. She recalled: 'It all happened in a matter of seconds, but I got a really good look at it. The sun was setting, and it was shining right on it. It had a really shiny coat and a big tail. It saw me and then slinked off into the hedge.'

Interestingly, it transpired that a neighbour of June Fooks – Anne Downing – had seen a similar creature in Rendlesham Forest around eighteen months previously. She explained: 'I was coming along a pathway with my daughter and saw this black animal in the distance. It was almost in a pouncing position and, when we got too near, it simply fled into the bush.'

Larry Warren, a former U.S. Air Force employee, a key witness to the out-of-this-world UFO events of December 1980 in Rendlesham Forest, and the co-author with Peter Robbins of the book *Left at East Gate* – which chronicles Warren's involvement in the case – also recalls some strange, paranormal-style activity within Rendlesham Forest during the time that he was stationed at nearby RAF Bentwaters.

There were, says Warren, dark tales of witchcraft and of druidism in the area; and then there was the story of the 'Lady without a Face' – a ghostly character said to ride a phantom bicycle along the lonely road that connected RAF Bentwaters with RAF Woodbridge, and who would scare the life out of anyone that dared to cross her path. But the most famous story that Warren heard while stationed at the base was that of 'East End Charlie', a spectral figure from the Second World War.

In Warren's own words: 'Rumour had it he was a German Luftwaffe pilot who had had the misfortune of being shot down near Woodbridge during the Battle of Britain. When irate townspeople caught him, they burned him alive. Now his ghost walks the flight line of Woodbridge and is said to be quite playful. I never saw him but was told he sat on the hood [bonnet] of the base fire department's patrol vehicle and burned his handprints into the metal.'

It is ironic that those who are sceptical of the Rendlesham Forest UFO case of December 1980 suggest that the airmen who were involved merely mistook the illumination from the nearby Orford Lighthouse for something more exotic. Why? Well, Orford itself is a veritable hotbed of weirdness and wild creatures. Consider, for example, the following account of Ralph of Coggershall. Recorded in the year 1200 in *Chronicon Anglicanum*, it describes the remarkable capture in the area of a wild-man-of-the-woods-style creature:

> 'In the time of King Henry II, when Bartholomew de Glanville was in charge of the castle at Orford, it happened that some fishermen fishing in the sea there caught in their nets a Wildman. He was naked and was like a man in all his members, covered with hair and with a long shaggy beard. He

eagerly ate whatever was brought to him, but if it was raw he pressed it between his hands until all the juice was expelled. He would not talk, even when tortured and hung up by his feet. Brought into church, he showed no sign of reverence or belief. He sought his bed at sunset and always remained there until sunrise. He was allowed to go into the sea, strongly guarded with three lines of nets, but he dived under the nets and came up again and again. Eventually he came back of his own free will. But later on he escaped and was never seen again.'

Without any shadow of a doubt, Rendlesham Forest – as well as its immediate surroundings – is a distinctly strange and surreal place. To paraphrase someone else's words: if you go down in the woods today, or indeed at any time, you really might be in for a big surprise!

Did Aliens Invade Britain 50 Years Ago?
2007

This was a question posed by me in a widely-published Net-based article of 2007 that was a kind of 'UFO anniversary' piece, as you'll see from the following words:

In May 2006, it was announced that after decades of secretly investigating UFOs, the Ministry of Defence had finally come to the conclusion that aliens were not visiting Britain. The MoD's assertions were revealed within the pages of a formerly classified document that had been commissioned in 1996 and that was completed in February 2000.

Titled the Condign Report, the 465-page document demonstrated how air defence experts had decided that UFO sightings were the result of 'natural, but relatively rare phenomena' such as ball-lightning and atmospheric plasmas. UFOs, wrote the still-unknown author of the MoD's report, were 'of no defence significance'.

Inevitably, Flying Saucer researchers accused the Ministry of covering up secrets of alien visitations to prevent public panic, and a debate began that continues to this day. And despite the Ministry's firm stance that ET is not invading our skies, it is an undeniable fact that not every case brought to the attention of defence officials can so easily be explained as those reports that were evaluated by the author of the Condign Report.

Indeed, 2007 marks the fiftieth anniversary of one of the most significant UFO cases ever investigated by the British Government. Moreover, as will become apparent, the official conclusion on the strange affair was that 'the incident was due to the presence of five reflecting objects of unknown type and origin' – which starkly conflicts with the findings of the Condign

Report.

It all began on the morning of April 4, 1957: according to the Royal Air Force's now-declassified documents housed at the National Archive, Kew, radar operators at Balscalloch, Scotland reported to RAF West Freugh, Wigtownshire that they had detected a number of 'unidentified objects on the screens of their radars'. And it quickly became apparent that this was no Cold War penetration of British airspace by Soviet spy-planes or bombers.

As the mystified radar-operators watched their screens, they were amazed to see a large, stationary object hovering at 50,000 feet that then proceeded to ascend vertically to no less than 70,000 feet. According to the files: 'A second radar was switched on and detected the object at the same range and height.'

The *X-Files*-style report continued:

> 'The unidentified object was tracked on the plotting table. After remaining at one spot for about 10 minutes the pen moved slowly in a NE direction, and gradually increased speed. A speed check was taken which showed a ground speed of 70 mph, the height was then 54,000 feet.'

And further reports began to pour into military bases across Scotland, as the following extract reveals:

> 'At this time another radar station 20 miles away, equipped with the same type of radars, was asked to search for the object. [An] echo was picked up at the range and bearing given and the radar was locked on.'

In fact, it appears that there were multiple UFOs in the area, as the RAF made clear in its report to the Air Ministry at Whitehall:

> 'After the object had travelled about 20 miles it made a very sharp turn and proceeded to move SE at the same increasing speed. Here the reports of the two radar stations differ in details. The two at Balscalloch tracked an object at about 50,000 feet at a speed of about 240 mph while the other followed an object or objects at 14,000 feet. As the objects travelled towards the second radar site the operators detected four objects moving in line astern about 4,000 yards from each other. This observation was confirmed later by the other radars.'

Most significant of all at this stage was the assessment by the radar experts of the incredible proportions of the UFOs:

> 'It was noted by the radar operators that the sizes of the echoes were considerably larger than would be expected from normal aircraft. In fact they considered that the size was nearer that of a ship's echo.'

And the Government's thoughts on the affair make for extraordinary reading:

> 'It is deduced from these reports that altogether five objects were detected by the three radars. Nothing can be said of physical construction except that they must have been either of considerable size or else constructed to be especially good reflectors.'

But is it possible that aircraft or balloons were to blame? Radar experts thought not:

> 'There were not known to be any aircraft in the vicinity nor were there any meteorological balloons. Even if balloons had been in the area these would not account for the sudden change of direction and the movement at high speed against the prevailing wind.'

The military also addressed the possibility that cloud formations might have produced a spurious radar report. But, again, this was summarily ruled out:

> 'Another point which has been considered is that the type of radar used is capable of locking onto heavily charged clouds. Cloud of this nature could extend up to the heights in question and cause abnormally large echoes on the radar screens. It is not thought however that this incident was due to such phenomena.'

And in a final, two-sentence statement, the Government came to a remarkable, out-of-this-world conclusion:

> 'The incident was due to the presence of five reflecting objects of unknown type and origin. It is considered unlikely that they were conventional aircraft, meteorological balloons or charged clouds.'

There ends the extraordinary report. That the West Freugh case mystified the military of 1957 was something that caused the Air Ministry a considerable amount of unease – even more so when it became apparent that the national media of the time had uncovered details of the story. Witness the following 'Secret' report prepared by the Air Ministry's Deputy Directorate of Intelligence:

> 'It is unfortunate that the Wigtownshire radar incident fell into the hands of the press. The two other radar incidents have not been made public and reached us by means of official secret channels. We suggest that Secretary of State does not specifically refer to these incidents as radar sightings. We suggest that S. of S. might reply: "Of the fifteen incidents reported this year, ten have been identified as conventional objects, two contain insufficient information for identification and three are under investigation."'

On April 17, 1957 Stan Awbery, Labour Member of Parliament for the city of Bristol, raised the issue of UFOs with Secretary of State for Air, George Ward. Awbery asked:

> 'What recent investigations have been made into unidentified flying objects; what photographs have been taken; and what reports have been made on this subject?'

In his reply, George Ward stated that:

> 'Reports are continually being received, and we investigate them wherever the details are sufficient. Most of the objects turn out to be balloons or meteors. One photograph recently received some publicity but was faked.'

Why Ward did not inform Awbery of the then-recent – and highly-credible - incident at West Freugh, Scotland is something of a mystery. That is unless one takes the view that the encounter was deemed so sensitive by the Air Ministry that the non-disclosure of information to elected members of the British Parliament was thought justified.

Despite the conclusions of the Condign Report and the Ministry of Defence's best efforts to deny that anything unusual is afoot in British airspace, it seems that the truth might be out there, after all…

MJ12, UFOs and the FBI 2007

Who could forget that 2007 marked the 20th anniversary of the surfacing of the beyond-dubious MJ12 documents? Well, I wish I could have forgotten that less-than-impressive anniversary. Sadly, I'm blessed (or cursed, in the case of MJ12) with a good memory; and so, when the hot summer of '07 rolled around, I just knew that those allegedly (but actually not) leaked, Top Secret government files were destined to once again darken my path. And, darken my path they most certainly did – in the form of an article I titled *MJ12, UFOs and the FBI*, and which was circulated across the Net in the summer of that year:

Amazingly, next month will mark the 20th anniversary of the first public airing (in Timothy Good's book *Above Top Secret*) of the so-called MJ12 documents that captured the imagination and attention of the entire ufological field for years. Indeed, for some – such as Stan Friedman – that attention is just as strong today as it ever was.

There have been arguments, counter-arguments and more with respect to the MJ12 papers, and the issue of whether they are – or are not – prime evidence for the existence of a super-secret group established during the President Harry Truman administration, and that had access to alien bodies and materials recovered at Roswell, New Mexico in July 1947.

The true believers continue to truly believe. And the arch-skeptics continue to…er…"arch-scoff." Let's raise a glass to the fact that we will still be debating MJ12 in another 20 years; and yes: the believers will still believe; and the skeptics will still scoff. Yet another aspect of the UFO mystery will remain utterly unresolved to the satisfaction of whatever remains of the

UFO research community of 2027.

And let's look forward to many more questions, comments, observations, glowing support and outright condemnation of an MJ12 kind…but no firm answers at all. Because that's what ufology is all about! It defies explanation and always remains tantalizingly elusive. Such was the name of the game when Keyhoe, Stringfield and their ilk were at the top of their game. Such is the game now. And such will be the game when, in the year 2293, the 196th book on the Roswell incident is published.

Given that I'll be 62 in 2027 (what a depressing thought…and I bet I will have lost my luxuriant and impressive head of hair by then, too), I sincerely hope that I am not writing a post at this very site that says: "Amazingly, next month will mark the 40th anniversary of the first public airing of…blah, blah, blah."

However, I have a horrible, nagging suspicion that I will be…

To the guys in the Intelligence world: tell us the truth! Twenty years of debating those accursed papers is enough torture for anyone!

It makes complete sense, after all, because then we'll leave you alone; you won't have to keep answering endless Freedom of Information Act requests from die-hard UFO researchers; and we can all move on to the Kennedy assassination, or the death of Princess Di, or something else that will never be resolved to everyone's satisfaction.

Let's face it: it can't be much fun for those that are sitting on top of the secret of Roswell (whatever the hell that may be!). Sixty years ago they were quite possibly akin to being the closest thing you could find to the *X-Files*' sinister and powerful Cigarette-Smoking Man. But today they're relegated to merely hanging out with the audiences at UFO conference-after-UFO conference, quietly and clandestinely listening to lecture-after-lecture about those damned and dastardly documents.

No wonder the Men in Black never smile. Would you if you were in their shoes?

Island of Paradise 2008

I first crossed paths with Stuart Miller back in 2005, when he was running the *UFO Review* website, and approached me for an interview on the subject of my then-new book, *Body Snatchers in the Desert* – a title that got whole swathes of the UFO research community all hot and bothered when it was published. On first speaking with Stuart I was very pleased to find that he was a man with a fine, and slightly subversive, sense of humor, a keen bullshit-detector, and a good appreciation of Ufology, its attendant absurdities, and pathetic egos-run-riot.

Dana and I hung out with Stuart for a weekend in 2006, when he held a conference in the city of Manchester on all-things-paranormal; and a good time was had by one and all. A year or so later, Stuart embarked upon a truly ambitious project: namely, one designed to once again put a ufological, colour, glossy magazine on the newsstands of the green and pleasant land of Great Britain. And, to the surprise of many – and to the anger and petty jealousies of some - he succeeded, albeit unfortunately very briefly, with *Alien Worlds*. I prepared a number of articles for *AW*, on a wide range of topics of a UFO-related nature; but I also did quite a bit of book-reviewing as well, including the following review of *Island of Paradise*: the 2008 margaritas-and-monsters-dominated masterpiece of the editor of this very book, Jonny-boy, himself, the Squire of Woolsery, the Dark-Lord of Devonshire, etc., etc:

As someone who is themselves an author, I am often asked to write reviews of other people's books. And so, when *Alien Worlds'* editor, the good (most of the time, at least) Mr. Miller, asked me if I would be willing to review the latest mighty tome from British writer, crypto-zoologist, and director of the Devon-based Centre for Fortean Zoology, Jonathan Downes, I immediately said yes.

Reviewing Jon's book, *Island of Paradise* – which is an on-the-road, warts-and-all, study of a week-long expedition to Puerto Rico in 2004 in search of the infamous Chupacabras – was somewhat of a departure for me; and I'll tell you why.

The vast majority of all the books I review are focused upon the adventures and exploits of other people. *Island of Paradise*, however, is very different; in the sense that it's a book in which I play a central role. Nevertheless, I hope this has not influenced my opinion of the book!

It was in the summer of 2004 that Jon and I headed off to the rain-forests of Puerto Rico, courtesy of the *Sci-Fi Channel*, who wanted to film us chasing the Chupacabras and UFOs for its now-defunct show *Proof Positive* – which was a pretty well executed combination of *The X-Files* meets *CSI*, albeit in a non-fiction format.

For seven days we rampaged and roamed around the island in search of the vampire-like beast, and heard tale after tale of crashed UFOs, dead aliens, bizarre conspiracies linking the Chupacabras with extra-terrestrial experimentation, secret military operations, black 'Flying Triangles', and much more. And, thanks to Jon, the whole story of that distinctly bizarre week is now finally chronicled in print.

The best way I can describe *Island of Paradise* is as a Fortean version of Hunter S. Thompson's fabulous *The Rum Diary* that told of the master's own journalistic adventures on Puerto Rico back in the 1950s.

Jon skilfully captures the essence of what makes Puerto Rico so magical, in terms of its history, its culture, its people - and its overwhelming weirdness, too. Truly, as Jon demonstrates, Puerto Rico is a locale that attracts the adventurer and the thrill-seeker like no other. And given that it was a veritable hot-bed of activity of the ufological, vampiric and downright uncanny kind, what else could I, or indeed we, do but welcome the aforementioned weirdness with wide-open arms.

If Jon and I were going to spend a week hunting vampires and/or aliens courtesy of the *Sci-Fi Channel*, then, as he reveals, there was no better place to do it than deep within the heart of the island of paradise, and while regularly fuelled by the finest of local cuisine and a plentiful supply of ever-present chilled margaritas and imported beer. Onward!

Having digested Jon's book, I can safely say that one thing stands out more than any other: only an adventure involving the Centre for Fortean Zoology could result in a deep discussion of *Fireball XL5*, Earl Grey Tea, Guantanamo Bay, Chupacabras DNA, Roswell, and the United States' ominous Department of Homeland Security!

I was pleased to see that Jon included in the pages of his book a description of our time spent at our base of operations: the *Wind Chimes* hotel in downtown San Juan. For those who weren't there, it might seem superfluous; but for Jon and me it was a time to rekindle a friendship that had been separated by the Atlantic for a couple of years; and it was a time to make new friendships with the *Sci-Fi Channel's* crew.

There is something unique about the camaraderie that comes with hanging out alongside fellow thrill-seekers and adventurers – all from different corners of the globe, most not even knowing each other, yet all thrust into a strange and surreal quest to seek out the truth about a diabolical beast said to roam a real-life paradise.

But, Jon demonstrates, it was without doubt the day we got our hands on a shining, silver Jeep that things really took off...

There's something special about driving around in an open-top Jeep in a place like Puerto Rico with one of your best friends, with the wind in your hair (for those who have hair...), and in hot pursuit of the unknown, while ear-splitting punk rock reverberates out of the CD player.

Barely one hour into our expedition, as Jon records, everything got a bit surreal. No expedition of this type would be complete without an excursion into the darkened depths of a shadowy old cave. That a bat decided to piss on my head while we were in there only made things more memorable. With much humour, Jon records how I decided not to bother with rabies injections of a type that Ozzy Osbourne was forced to undergo after his own legendary encounter with a bat; and instead I hoped that the little pisser wasn't rabid, and that I wouldn't wake up the next day like one of the frenzied souls from *28 Days Later* or the spectacular 2004 remake of *Dawn of the Dead*. Needless to say, I didn't.

Of course, I knew that all of this would serve as good fodder for Jon's planned book on our trip around the island, and so I merely wiped my head with my bandana, swore at the offending beast and his or her brethren and continued roaming and filming. And a crew of a dozen, led by the good Mr. Downes himself, laughed heartily!

Perhaps of most interest to readers of this magazine is what Jon has to say about an alleged UFO crash deep in the El Yunque rain-forest of Puerto Rico back in 1957. Jon tells the reader of our fascinating encounter with a woman named Norka who was able to fill in some of the gaps suggesting that at least *something* had genuinely crashed on Puerto Rico back in the 1950s, and who was also a veritable fountain of knowledge on all-things monstrous too. As long as I live, I will never forget that moment when Norka told us of her own personal encounter with the Chupacabras late one night in 1975, and Jon and I turned to each other and realised that the beast Norka had seen was practically identical to the notorious Owlman of England – a creature that Jon had hunted, and been haunted by, for years. It was truly a pivotal moment in that memorable week.

As we sat on the balcony of Norka's beautiful home high in the hills of El Yunque, sipping cold drinks, listening to her stories, and with the sun bathing down on us, I knew that we were experiencing something very special, and that beneath its beautiful exterior, something – or *some things* - dark, ominous, dangerous and bizarre dwelled on the island. And Jon's chapter on this particular encounter most certainly does not disappoint.

One of the things that stood out for me upon reading *Island of Paradise* was how the initial quest quickly became something very different – and particularly so when new, and unforeseen, factors came into play. We had flown to Puerto Rico with the intention of trying to determine, for the benefit of the Sci-Fi Channel, if we could find, examine and identify any evidence for the existence of the Chupacabras – such as undeniable DNA. Yet, by the end of the week we were deeply immersed in stories of crashed UFOs, genetic mutation, bizarre changes in the island's ecology and much more.

I will never forget that week in the summer of 2004 when Jon and I roamed Puerto Rico's rain-forest, its lowlands and its little villages in search of monsters, UFOs and aliens. It was an experience that will stay with me for all my life, and one that (as the book records) was as much about friendship, adventures and good times as it was about hunting for the Chupacaras and for the remains of wrecked alien spacecraft. And at the end of the day, that was good enough for me. As for Jon: well, *Island of Paradise* tells it all, just as it was – the good, the bad and the plain strange.

If you're looking for the definitive book on the Chupacabras, its potential links with the UFO controversy in general (and crashed UFOs in particular), and what goes on behind the scenes of an on-site, week-long investigation in an exotic and mysterious world, then *Island of Paradise* is most definitely the one for you.

El Yunque, the home of the Goat-Sucker.

An Alien Who's Who 2008

And, then, there was this review from me for Stuart Miller's *Alien Worlds*: of *An Alien Who's Who*, which was a highly-entertaining and deadpan-funny title from Martin S. Kottmeyer that was published by the good chaps at Anomalist Books in 2008:

Depending on your own personal perspective regarding what lies at the heart of the UFO puzzle, *An Alien Who's Who* reveals a great deal about (a) the dizzying variety of extraterrestrials that have visited the Earth for a good many years; (b) the tall-tales of a whole range of fantasists and con-merchants; or (c) the way in which the UFO phenomenon, and those within it, are constantly being manipulated and exploited by a true trickster of a type that would make both John Keel and Jacques Vallee very proud. Or, maybe it's all three theories, or perhaps none of them. Whatever the case, I know only this much for certain: Martin Kottmeyer's book is damned good fun and highly informative – and in equal measures, too.

Basically, it's a 263-page, A to Z-style page-turner that lists a truly startling number of names attributed to aliens that are said to have visited the Earth. Of course, reading about the trials, tribulations and exploits of hundreds of alleged aliens that range from Acorc (the denizen of an over-crowded planet 52 million kilometers from Earth) to Zyloo (who supposedly 'followed Apollo 13' and became involved in the 'Sixth Patrol Division', whatever the hell that is or was) could very quickly become tedious.

In the hands of Kottmeyer, however, tediousness is the last thing that springs to mind. Certainly, most of the entries are relatively brief; however, they are also tinged with a welcome bit of deadpan humour. For example, Herronoah – who hails from the planet Epicot - tells a startled earthling named 'Edwin W' that human beings wear too many clothes, and goes on to inform Edwin how, on one occasion, 'their ship spooked a naked woman and man in a clump of bushes'. Ahem.

Then we get treated to the spectacle of Aura Rhanes, the hot space-babe from a far-off world called Clarion who, according to Truman Bethurum, the man she appeared before, wore 'slacks' that 'appeared almost as if painted on her, so snugly did they fit'. Lucky Truman, that's all I can say. And what are we to make of Motag, who 'once converted a flying saucer into a truck'? Or Nokyle, who intriguingly threatens to reveal details of a certain incident involving what are tantalisingly described only as 'crazy girls'?

As you have probably already guessed, many of the entries contained within the packed pages of *An Alien Who's Who* hail from that much-ridiculed era of the so-called Contactee: those seemingly elite souls who claimed face-to-face encounters with long-haired aliens back in the 1950s and whose names were invariably made up of a lot of Q's, Z's and X's.

It should be stressed that the ridiculous and often hysterical nature of some of the stories does not undermine Kottmeyer's credibility as an author. Indeed, he points out in his Introduction that he does not believe in 'physically real aliens', from Venus, Mars, Pluto, and so on.

Rather, for the most part, Kottmeyer has done something that few authors seldom do: he leaves his own views and beliefs at the door, and instead provides the reader with entertaining – and otherwise very hard to find – summaries on alleged other-worldly entities that have supposedly been manifesting before select members of the Human Race for decades.

Kottmeyer relates their bizarre, unverifiable and at times completely false tales, prophecies and warnings. And, in a roundabout way, he amply demonstrates that for all the attempts to legitimise Ufology as a serious science, it is still a subject that is packed with odd and unusual characters with weird names and even weirder motivations – and if you think I'm just talking about the aliens here, well, you're very wrong, my friends.

With an entertaining and insightful Foreword from ufologist and *Project Beta* author Greg Bishop, *An Alien Who's Who* is vital reading for anyone and everyone that wants to learn more about some of the strange, other-worldly beings said to have visited our planet and whose exploits, without Kottmeyer, would otherwise be lost to the fog of time.

And, with all that now said, I'm off to meet Solar-Commander Xzzobovaxxx for a spot of dinner, followed by a flight around Venus with the bikini-clad Amazonians of Delta-Zorvog 12. Wish me luck!

The Missing Chapter 2008

In 2008, Anomalist Books published my title *There's something in the Woods* – which, basically, was a diary-style book covering my investigations of cryptozoological critters, crashed UFOs, crop circles and much more in the period from spring 2006 to early 2008. Patrick Huyghe, the editor, liked the book very much; however, there was one chapter he wasn't so keen on – and so it never saw the light of day. A cold-hearted and utterly-lethal Patrick deleted that very same chapter; he exterminated it from the face of the planet, even. Okay, I have to confess I'm slightly exaggerating here: it wasn't so much that Patrick didn't actually like the chapter (he really did!). Rather, whereas all of the other chapters in the book chronicled my on-the-road investigations, the elusively-missing one was a write-up of my weird experiences at conferences, gigs and airports – on both sides of the Atlantic. Patrick felt - and with hindsight, I have to agree with him now – that it seemed out-of-place when placed against the rest of the material. Finally, however, here it is. Originally titled *Weekends of Weirdness*, the chapter is a strange mix of conspiracy, Homeland Security agents, airport shenanigans, Hollywood movie-moguls and much more:

In early 2005, I was contacted, quite out of the blue, by a guy named Mike Kuciak. It transpired that Mike worked in Hollyweird, as I like to call that modern-day Sodom and Gomorrah, and had read my book *Three Men Seeking Monsters*. As I listened, and much to my complete and utter astonishment, Mike told me that his company, AEI, felt *Three Men* was not just highly entertaining reading: it would also make a great Hollywood movie.

Well, several of my other books, including *Body Snatchers in the Desert*, had been optioned by television companies, but nothing of any real substance had ever developed after the obligatory signing of contracts and selling of souls. As interested as I certainly was to hear what Mike had to say, my heart was hardly racing with excitement, given the past record of my involvement with the world of on-screen entertainment. Mike assured me, however, that if anyone could make such a project work, AEI could. And so, over the next few months, further discussion took place: between me, Mike, my literary agent, Lisa Hagan, and Sandra Martin, who was both the publisher of the book and Lisa's mother. As with my previous books, contracts were exchanged and there was a great deal of discussion and speculation about what might, or might not even, develop. I vowed not to get too excited until I saw my name up in lights on Hollywood Boulevard.

Imagine my surprise and shock when, in mid-2006, and shortly after gallivanting around the Cannock Chase's German Cemetery with Dana, I received an email from an excited Sandra, informing me that none other than Universal Studios had optioned the book. Not only that: Universal considered the book to be the perfect on-screen vehicle for upcoming Hollywood star, Jon Heder. That's right: according to the rumor-mill, *Napoleon Dynamite*, himself, was set to play me on the big-screen. "Can he put on a British accent, and is he willing to shave his head for the part?" I asked Sandra. Well, after digesting this extraordinary development, I quickly telephoned Jon Downes and Richard Freeman, my comrades-in-arms in *Three Men*, and informed them of what was going down. After almost-literally picking themselves up off the floor, Richard loudly pontificated that he would allow no-one but Johnny Depp to portray him on-screen; while Jon was practically ready to buy himself a tuxedo for a stroll down the red-carpet.

For the next year or so, negotiations continued, and it was in the summer of 2007 that everything was finalised to the satisfaction of all those involved. Coincidentally, on the day that the contract was signed, I received a transatlantic telephone call from Jon, asking if I was in a position to speak at his forthcoming annual *Weird Weekend* gig.

In Jon's language, "in a position" basically meant: could I pay my own airfare from the United States? The life of a struggling author meant that I could not. Jon - who was hardly in a financial position to cover my flight expenses, either - and I lamented the fact that it seemed we were destined not to hang out for a few days of mirth and merriment. Nevertheless, I did what I always do when situations call for drastic and unconventional measures: I meditated for a while, and dispatched into the great beyond a request for rapid assistance in getting me to the *Weird Weekend*, one way or another, and come hell or high water. And the great beyond not only listened: it well and truly delivered the goods.

Only forty-eight-hours before Jon's gig was set to kick-off, I had resigned myself to the fact that there was no way at all that I was going to have the opportunity to speak at the event and see my old mates again. But I should have had far more faith. While still cursing my bad luck, the telephone rang. It was Mike Kuciak: "Can you fly to England tomorrow? Universal want you there. Jon Heder's brother, Doug, and a guy named Mark Steven Johnson, who they've hired to write the *Three Men* screenplay, want you at the *Weird Weekend*. They want to hang out and chat with you, Jon and Richard. They'll pay for your flight and all your expenses."

I punched my fists into the air, thanked the ancient gods of synchronicity and fate, and quickly telephoned Jon to tell him the good news. The next day, with airline tickets having been emailed to me, I hastily crammed my trusty back-pack with several changes of clothing, bathroom accessories, books, cameras and more, and headed off to Dallas-Fort Worth Airport for a trip to the other side of the world. I was going to be at the *Weird Weekend*, after all.

The *Weird Weekend* is an affair that is always as odd as it is engaging and enthralling. I have said it before and I will say it again: if you are a pompous, self-important author who demands a room at the nearest *Holiday Inn*, a taxi to the gig and back, and banquet-style feasts, don't bother coming. If, however, you are like me and the various other faces of Forteana that regularly speak at Jon's gig, and you are willing to help out with the organizing, are prepared to spend your nights curled up in a sleeping-bag on Jon's living-room floor (or kitchen floor, in my case), and enjoy the life of a travelling, bohemian nomad, then this is the conference for you. But of all of the *Weird Weekend's* I have attended, the 2007 one was without doubt the most bizarre.

Given the fact that the village of Woolfardisworthy is hardly a large one, and is a place where not much of an extraordinary nature ever occurs, when rumours began to wildly spread about not just among the attendees at the *Weird Weekend*, but throughout the entire village too, that two Hollywood types were about to descend on this sleepy, Devonshire locale, a high degree of anticipation filled the air. Such anticipation filled me too: after all, I had not even met Doug and Mark, and I knew not a thing about them, aside from the fact that (a) Doug was one of the prime-movers in Greasy Entertainment, that was his brother Jon's production company; and (b) Mark had an illustrious career, was the producer of the movies *Grumpy Old Men* and *Daredevil* and was good friends with actor Nicolas Cage. Blimey!

After arriving at Heathrow Airport early on the Saturday morning, I quickly hired a car, and sped off down the M5 motorway to Woolfardisworthy. Having fought endless traffic jams, I finally arrived around 6.00 p.m., and amid much fanfare courtesy of Jon, who jumped around with wild glee at the sight of his old friend. Have you ever seen Jon jump around with wild glee? It is an extraordinary, slightly disturbing and unforgettable sight, to say the very least. Thankfully, Mark and Doug were very down to earth; and Mark plied me with endless pints of good old British beer as he, Doug, me, Jon and Richard chatted amiably about all-things of a *Three Men*-nature for an hour or two.

When the conversation with Doug and Mark was exhausted, Jon pulled me to one side and said quietly in my ear: "You won't believe this, mate; but we have been getting a load of reports of a huge black cat prowling around the area. A huge bugger: about eight feet long." He added quietly: "When you and Dana came down last year, and I said to you that all that messing around in the German Cemetery might have resulted in you bringing some of those beasts with you to my house, I may not have been wrong."

I expressed my amazement. Jon nodded grimly and related the facts: it was in the nearby Huddisford Woods that most of the action had taken place. One of the most intriguing cases, Jon told me as we sat in a quiet corner of his dining-room, came from a Mr. Harris who had telephoned him midway through July and divulged a remarkable tale of his own, and then-recent, encounter with the beast of the woods. Jon thrust into my hand a print-out of a Word document that Corinna, who accompanied Jon to both the home of the witness and the location of the encounter itself, had prepared on the affair and that read thus:

> "Just before 6.00 p.m., Mr. Harris had been disturbed by the loud squawking of his chickens in a field next to his home. From past experience, he recognized that their sudden loud calls meant there was something amiss, so he went to investigate. He saw a large animal lying down in some long grass under a low-growing tree, about twenty-five feet from where he was standing, and realized that it was no ordinary dog or cat. When it saw him, it bounded off across the field, in the general direction of the dense woods that bordered the area, but not before Mr. Harris identified it as a large black cat. He said he estimated it as being eight feet in length. He showed us where it had been laying. Under the tree there was a large area of flattened grass. It was obvious, by the tracks left in the long grass, where the animal had taken large strides across the field to escape its discovery. As it bounded away from him, Mr. Harris lost sight of it from where he was standing, but we followed the tracks. They were around twelve feet apart; and it seemed apparent that it had jumped through a hole in the hedgerow, which led straight into the darkness of the woods behind it."

Interestingly, Corinna had then written something that many witnesses to unknown beasts had reported in the past: namely, a feeling of distinct unease in those locations frequented by the creatures of the night. Corinna wrote:

> "There is also another place, quite close by, where several people have seen a big cat. We drove through it on our way home – a very eerie place. Nothing much to note about it. It's just a road that dips into a small valley, over a tiny Devonshire bridge, and then up again. However, there is something very unsettling about it. Driving through it, I felt quite anxious, almost to the point of the hairs standing up on the back of my neck. A minute or so later, after leaving the area, all felt well again. Very odd and not a place I would like to walk home by myself late at night. In fact, I would not even fancy driving through it by myself. It oozed a sense of doom. I wonder why that is? Strange how some areas can give you a real sense of dread as you pass through them, for no apparent reason at all."

I was just about to ask Jon where this mysterious location was, in the event that I had time to get out there for myself later that night, when we were sidetracked by someone who wanted our opinions on whether or not Dick Cheney had instigated 9-11. Unfortunately, and partly as a result of a jet-lagged brain and the chaos that is the *Weird Weekend*, I summarily forgot about the big cat of Woolfardisworthy.

A night of revelry followed, and continued until the early hours, when I finally hit the hay at Jon's, along with the rest of the speakers. Sunday morning and afternoon were spent hanging

Ghost-Hunter and good mate, Joshua P. Warren.

out with Mark and Doug, and lecturing to the *Weird Weekend* audience on the dark tales of the Cannock Chase Bigfoot. The day extended into a dinner at the local *Farmer's Arms* pub, and a late-night chat back at Jon's, as old friends who had not seen each other for a while caught up on news, gossip and more. And before I knew it, the rollercoaster-of-a-weekend was over. My travels and adventures were far from finished, however.

It was around 7.00 a.m. on the Monday morning when I woke up, distinctly bleary of eye. Not only that: barely thirty-six hours after arriving at Jon's, I was facing a five-hour car journey to Gatwick Airport, followed by a three-hour check-in, and then a long-haul, nine-hour flight back to Dallas. Given the fact that I felt like one of the living dead, I was hardly looking forward to the drive to the airport – particularly as the sprinkling of rain that fell the previous night had turned into a typically British downpour of truly torrential proportions; and keeping my eyes open even now was a torturous task, to say the very least.

I decided to pack my bags, make a pot of hot tea and plates of buttery toast for me and UFO author Larry Warren, who was also just rising from the depths of his sleeping-bag, and then hit the road – lest I drift off into the arms of Morpheus and remain forever stranded at Jon's. Before saying my goodbyes to Larry, I left a hastily-scribbled note in Jon's office (he and Corinna were still deep in slumber – or something - upstairs) saying that it was great to see him and his good wife again, and thanking them for their fine hospitality over the course of the weekend. And then I was gone. The road, as always, was beckoning.

As my return flight was luckily one without connections, I got my head down for about seven hours and woke up fully refreshed and revitalized just before the plane hit the runway at DFW Airport. Given the fact that I had only taken a back-pack with me for the two-and-a-half days that I was in England, I anticipated that negotiating Customs would be a breeze. How utterly wrong I was.

I arrived at Customs, where a stern-faced automaton asked me: "Where's your luggage?"

"This is it," I replied, good-naturedly. "I was only gone three days and didn't see the point of hauling a big case when I could stuff everything into a small bag."

The automaton eyed me suspiciously and took another look at my passport and residency card. He then pointed to the right of me and said in icy and ominous tones: "Sir, you will follow that line, where you will be met by another customs officer."

"For Christ's sake," I moaned, "I deliberately took a small bag to avoid getting hassle, and now I'm getting hassle! All that's in it is a couple of changes of clothes, half-a-dozen books, a tube of toothpaste and a roll-on deodorant!"

The man was not impressed: "Sir, there is an easy way to do this and there is a hard way to do it, too." He carefully looked at his watch and added: "For exactly the next sixty seconds, the easy option is still open to you." I shook my head, utterly exasperated, and made my way through another door, like the cow to the slaughter-house, to learn the nature of the dark fate that awaited me. On doing so, I was ushered into a further room, where I was told, by yet another curiously similar breed of unsmiling automaton, to place my bag on a table and very slowly and very carefully open it. Utterly unimpressed by my welcoming committee, I did so.

"You travelled to England with nothing except a back-pack?" the man asked.

"Yeah, I just told your colleague that I was literally only gone for three days – and that included travelling time! I stuffed this bag with clothes and all I'd need, because for a total of just seventy-two hours I didn't need anymore!"

"Lower your voice, sir. So, why were you in England for only three days?"

"I was speaking at a conference," I said, through gritted teeth.

The man's eyebrows rose significantly: "And what was the subject matter of the conference?"

"Bigfoot," I replied, matter-of-factly.

"Bigfoot?" he echoed, with puzzlement.

"Bigfoot," I repeated. I pulled out a copy of my *Man-Monkey* book from my bag and thrust it in front of his face.

"One moment, sir," was his ominous, three-word response. This is it, I thought: I'm about to be whisked off to yet another room, and out will come the rubber-gloves and an interrogation courtesy of an unsmiling soul from the Department of Homeland Security or the FBI. Instead, something distinctly different, and very welcoming, happened.

Across the length of the room the man shouted to a colleague, who was busy rummaging through some other, poor soul's case: "Hey, this guy writes books about Bigfoot!"

"Bigfoot?" his puzzled colleague replied.

My interrogator bellowed in return: "You know: Sasquatch!"

"Alright!" came the genial reply, and the man came galloping over, as did another inquisitive official. And, with my little bag returned to me amid a surprisingly fawning, but very welcome, apology for having been detained, I spent the next few minutes engaged in a deep chat about all things beast-like and hairy with a group of special-agents of the United States' Government. Questions about Bigfoot footprints and plaster-casts, photos, witness accounts and more bombarded me; while I did my best to answer them, amid an atmosphere that was as unreal as it was surreal.

It was only when an old, blue-haired lady in the line behind me began to complain loudly that the aforementioned agents should be attending to her, instead of chatting about Bigfoot "with someone who isn't even an American," that the conversation came to an abrupt end. The trio thanked me for my time, promised to buy their own copies of *Three Men Seeking Monsters* and wished me well in my future expeditions and adventures. On the way out, I caught sight of the original agent who had insisted I do it the easy way or the hard way. I waved genially in his direction and gave him the thumbs-up as I exited Dallas-Fort Worth Airport. He merely glared back, in the fashion that only airport officials, and Taser-wielding cops, can.

Midway through 2006, ghost-hunter, author and paranormal investigator Josh Warren contacted me with a proposal, and it was a good one, too. As Josh correctly put it, there were countless conferences held every year on UFOs, crypto-zoology and conspiracy theories. But all of them were very much static and staid affairs, stuck in the same hotel, in the same city, year after year. So, said Josh: "Are you interested in getting on-board with me and Jim Marrs and trying to do a paranormal tour? I'd speak on ghosts; Jim would do conspiracies; and you could do monsters."

"Like a rock-band hitting the road, you mean?" I replied.

"Exactly!" said Josh loudly and with a laugh in his voice. I said that, yes, I most certainly was interested. And thus was borne the *Dark 30 Tour* – so named after a term describing those early hours of the morning when distinct high-strangeness begins to raise its dark and foreboding head. I knew Jim well – he lived barely an hour's drive from my Dallas home. As for Josh, I had worked with him, and Jim too, in the latter part of 2005 on a UFO documentary for the Discovery Channel, and we soon became good friends. In other words, we had an ideal line-up for the tour. It kicked off in fine form in Kansas City in early December 2006; however, it was the leg of the tour held in Josh's hometown of Asheville, North Carolina in late September 2007 that was particularly memorable.

Somehow, I just knew that the weekend in Asheville was going to be a distinctly weird one. Hell, even the days leading up to it were odd, to say the very least. It was mid-afternoon on September 26, the day before I flew out to Asheville to meet up with Josh and Jim, when good friend and fellow researcher Greg Bishop telephoned me from deep in the heart of the Californian desert to say that he was – quite literally as we spoke - being spied upon by a remotely-controlled U.S. Air Force *Predator* drone aircraft that was circling ominously and menacingly above him.

A highly concerned Greg backtracked and explained the facts: my literary agent, Lisa Hagan, of Paraview Books, had left a voice-mail with Greg earlier that day to explain that *Fox News* was looking to speak with him about his UFO research. But there was a problem: Lisa had forgotten to leave her telephone number and it wasn't showing up on Greg's cell-phone either. And so, while hanging out in the barren Californian desert and soaring around the hot, midday skies in his micro-light, Greg decided to call me on his cell-phone to ask if I had Lisa's office number at hand. Fortunately, I did.

But there was another problem, too: Greg didn't have a pen or paper handy. Then he had a thought: why not write it in big letters on the desert floor? And so, as I sat sprawled on the couch in my Dallas apartment and related the number down the telephone, Greg duly landed his flying machine, quickly fell to his hands and knees and began scrawling amidst the hot desert dust, the cacti and the rattlesnakes.

"Got it?" I asked.

"Yeah, thanks. I'll program it in my phone now," he replied, adding in slightly concerned tones: "That drone's still flying around."

I said in response: "What the hell do you expect, mate? They probably know full well who you are, and now they think you're writing down coded messages in the sand. You know you're going to be public enemy number one at this rate, don't you?"

Greg laughed: "What's weird is that earlier today, Sigrid [Greg's girlfriend] gave me a couple of books from the library she works at that they were going to throw out."

"What's wrong with that?" I asked, puzzled.

"Well...they were on explosives," Greg told me, his voice dropping to a concerned whisper.

"Ah," I said, in conspiratorial tones, "that explains it: books on explosives and now you're out in the desert with your flying machine and right where the military is parading its *Predator* around the skies. They've probably got some high power-camera focused on the phone-number you've just written in the desert, too."

"Why would they do that?" Greg asked me.

I explained, while sipping on a wonderful, icy mix of vodka and mango juice: "That just happens to be the phone number of a major publisher of books on conspiracy theories, UFOs and the paranormal. The Men in Black who are remotely-flying that *Predator* are probably shitting a brick right now what with all this talk of explosives, *Fox News*, conspiracy publishers, you in your plane, scrawling numbers on the desert floor, and phoning me. And I'll bet my balls they've already traced the number, too."

"Ah, yes..." Greg replied, before drifting off into silence.

"Keep a look out for that *Predator*, Greg. And watch your back," I added, only half in jest.

"I will," he assured me. "Bye; and thanks." The phone went dead. Greg went back to evading sinister characters in the Californian desert, while I returned to my vodka and mango juice and an afternoon spent packing clothes, books, and other sundry items for my flight to Asheville, North Carolina where I was due to lecture on my favorite topics of werewolves, ape-men, lake-monsters, and bat-winged gargoyles.

The weekend was great fun, with much merry-making, gadding about town checking out the local pubs and haunted locales, and lecturing for the hundred or so people who turned up to hear me, Josh and Jim speak. Not only that: the event was held at the Asheville Pizza and Brewing Company: hell, it doesn't get much better than that! And on a crypto-zoological front it was highly intriguing. As Josh and one of his friends, Micah, told me, the area was a well-known haunt for mysterious big-cats, even though at an official level it was summarily denied that such beasts roamed historic Asheville and the surrounding countryside.

The most interesting story, however, came from a member of the audience: a woman of about forty who told me how, as a teenager in 1982, and while hiking through the state's glorious Blue Ridge Mountains with her parents, she – and they - had briefly seen in a clearing at a distance of about two hundred feet what appeared to be a giant, hairy, man-like beast.

"Are you sure it wasn't a bear?" I asked. The woman smiled knowingly and told me she was sure of three things only. First: no, it was not a bear. Second: it was a huge and hairy ape-like man. And, third: its fur was dazzling white in color. Well, this latter point was of particular interest to me. Although most reports described Bigfoot as having dark-brown or black fur, occasionally stories of white Bigfoot did surface. The woman admitted to me that the creature was only in sight for a very few seconds, but it was certainly long enough for her to get a decent look at it. She didn't want to elaborate, declined to speak on the record, but had several memorable parting words for me: "Whatever people might say, I can tell you this: Bigfoot lives on the Blue Ridge Mountains."

On the day after the gig, Josh, his wife, Lauren, and I headed up into the mountains; and I confess that I felt a tinge of excitement at what might be lurking within those dense trees. Sadly, we saw nothing of a monstrous nature, but I elected to one day return and spend a night or two out in the wilds of North Carolina – just in case.

Manipulating the Crashed UFO Scene 2009

I've known UFO researcher, writer and blogger Rich Reynolds for a number of years now, and consider him a fine researcher and friend; and I've written more than a few articles for his blog: *The UFO Iconoclast(s)*; including one in 2009 titled *Manipulating the Crashed UFO Scene*. The article kind of followed on from my *Body Snatchers in the Desert* book; in the sense that it offered additional data suggesting that the UFO research community had been (and continues to be) well and truly played by U.S. intelligence in relation to the notion that UFOs have crashed to earth. It reads thus:

Have UFOs crashed to earth?

Was Roswell 'real'?

Have alien bodies been retrieved and autopsied?

Many people certainly believe so. Even I ('The Scourge of Roswell') used to believe so. And there's something else, too; something surprising: key elements of the official world want you to believe that UFOs have crashed. They're pleased you believe. They rub their hands together in secret glee as they congratulate themselves on a job well-done.

Yes: it's truly ironic that those same key elements may well be up to their collective necks in crashed UFO tales - but there's a possibility that none of them may have any basis in literal

UFO reality whatsoever.

Instead, there is good evidence that the collective UFO research community may have been the unwitting victim of a huge con-trick; one designed to (a) hide classified military ops under a crashed UFO banner; and (b) control and manipulate a group of people (namely us) that the official world perceives as being (at times, at least) troublesome and a potential threat to national security.

So, with that said, where do we begin? Where else: the early years of the UFO, the 1940s.

Psychological Saucers:
It's worth noting (mainly because few have bothered to note it, or to understand and appreciate the significance of the matter) that one of the "Recommendations" of a lengthy Technical Report prepared by the Air Force's flying saucer study, Project Grudge, way back in August 1949, states: "That Psychological Warfare Division and other governmental agencies interested in psychological warfare be informed of the results of this study."

The Department of Defence's official definition of psychological warfare is: "The planned use of propaganda and other psychological actions having the primary purpose of influencing the opinions, emotions, attitudes, and behaviour of hostile foreign groups in such a way as to support the achievement of national objectives."

As the above Grudge revelations show, way back when in the formative years of Ufology, certain players were looking to understand how the subject could be used psychologically.

Saucers and the CIA:
A 1952 document from then-CIA director Walter B. Smith to the Director of the Psychological Strategy Board, titled "Flying Saucers," states: "I am today transmitting to the National Security Council a proposal in which it is concluded that the problems connected with unidentified flying objects appear to have implications for psychological warfare as well as for intelligence and operations. I suggest that we discuss at an early board meeting the possible offensive or defensive utilization of these phenomena for psychological warfare purposes."

According to Gerald Haines, historian for the National Security Agency and the CIA, in the early 1950s,

> "The CIA...searched the Soviet press for UFO reports, but found none, causing the group to conclude that the absence of reports had to have been the result of deliberate Soviet Government policy. The group also envisioned the USSR's possible use of UFOs as a psychological warfare tool. In addition, they worried that, if the US air warning system should be deliberately overloaded by UFO sightings, the Soviets might gain a surprise advantage in any nuclear attack. Because of the tense Cold War situation and increased Soviet capabilities, the CIA Study Group saw serious national security concerns in the flying saucer situation. The group believed that the Soviets could use

UFO reports to touch off mass hysteria and panic in the United States. The group also believed that the Soviets might use UFO sightings to overload the US air warning system so that it could not distinguish real targets from phantom UFOs."

Significantly, the CIA Study Group

"did find that continued emphasis on UFO reporting might threaten 'the orderly functioning' of the government by clogging the channels of communication with irrelevant reports and by inducing 'hysterical mass behaviour' harmful to constituted authority. The panel also worried that potential enemies contemplating an attack on the United States might exploit the UFO phenomena and use them to disrupt US air defences."

This, in essence, is the CIA's official stance with respect to the UFO puzzle. The CIA was most concerned about the way in which the Soviets might exploit the UFO subject as a tool of psychological warfare and spread bogus UFO accounts to clog intelligence channels. In other words, it was not UFOs per se that particularly interested or alarmed the CIA, but the way in which the subject itself could be manipulated for other, more novel purposes.

As we shall now see, it was during these formative years that the American intelligence community began to realize how it, too might make use of the crashed UFO mystery to further muddy the waters concerning the incidents in New Mexico in 1947.

And so it was that, in the late 1940s and early 1950s, several crashed UFO tales surfaced – all of which bore the hallmarks of official involvement, both in their creation and dissemination.

The Aztec Affair:

Next to the so-called Roswell Incident of July 1947, certainly the most talked-about "UFO crash" of all is that which is alleged to have occurred in the vicinity of Aztec, New Mexico, in 1948.

According to information related to the author Frank Scully in the late 1940s, and subsequently published in his best-selling 1950 book, *Behind the Flying Saucers*, the wreckage of four alien spacecraft, and no fewer than 34 alien bodies, had been recovered by American authorities as a result of a number of separate incidents in 1947 and 1948, and were being studied under cover of the utmost secrecy at defence establishments in the United States.

Scully was willing to admit that the bulk of his information had come from two primary sources: Silas Mason Newton, who was described in a 1941 FBI report as a 'wholly unethical businessman,' and one 'Dr. Gee', the name given to protect eight scientists, all of whom had supposedly divulged various details of the crashes to Newton and Scully. According to Scully's sources one such UFO was found in Hart Canyon, near the town of Aztec, in March 1948.

After the Aztec saucer had crashed, said Scully, it was found essentially intact by elements of the military that gained access to the object via a fractured porthole. Inside they found the bodies of no fewer than sixteen small, human-like creatures, all slightly charred and undoubtedly dead. The UFO was then dismantled and the bodies of the crew were transferred to Wright Field, Dayton, Ohio for study.

At the time of its release, Scully's book caused a major sensation. In both 1952 and 1953, however, J. P. Cahn, a reporter who had previously worked for the San Francisco Chronicle, authored two detailed exposes, which cast serious doubt on the claims of Newton and 'Dr. Gee' – identified not as 'eight scientists' but as one Leo Gebauer, who had a background as equally dubious as that of Newton.

Yet, as the years have shown, the Aztec crashed UFO incident refuses to roll over and die – indeed it has now spawned a whole industry.

Even today, the Aztec story continues to perplex and intrigue: a fascinating piece of documentary evidence relative to the Aztec case surfaced in the late 1990s, thanks to the late investigative author Karl Pflock – and it is one that may ultimately shed more light on the psychological warfare angle of the crashed UFO mystery.

"In 1998, under curious circumstances," stated Pflock,

> "I was made privy to a fascinating document about one of the most controversial cases of the Golden Age of Flying Saucers, the so-called Aztec crash of 1948. I had little more than passing interest in the case until 1998, when a source, who insists on complete anonymity, showed me a handwritten testament, set down by the key player in this amazing, often amusing, truth-is-stranger-than-fiction episode.
>
> "[I]t seems that what I was shown was...something penned by sly old Silas Newton, but what can we say about the veracity of its content? After the Denver Post revealed he was Scientist X, Newton received two visitors at his Newton Oil Company office in Denver. These men claimed to be with a highly secret U.S. Government entity, which they refused to name. Were they Air Force OSI agents, who Newton hyped into something more mysterious? Newton writes, 'They grilled me, tried to poke holes in my story. Had no trouble doing it and laughed in my face about the scientific mistakes I made. They never said so, but I could tell they were trying to find out if I really knew anything about flying saucers that had landed. Did not take those fellows long to decide I did not. But I sure knew they did.'"

Pflock expands further and the tale becomes decidedly intriguing: "Newton's visitors told him they knew he was pulling a scam and then gave him what may have been the surprise of his life.

> 'Those fellows said they wanted me to keep it up, keep telling the flying

saucer story and that they and the people they worked for would look out for me and for Leo. I could just go on doing what I always did and not worry about it.'"

Pflock asks:
"Did the U.S. Government or someone associated with it use Newton to discredit the idea of crashed flying saucers so a real captured saucer or saucers could be more easily kept under wraps? Was this actually nothing to do with real saucers but instead some sort of psychological warfare operation?"

Klondike and the Crown

And then there is Operation Klondike. Following the collapse of Nazi Germany, several of Hungary's national treasures, including the Crown of St. Stephen, were handed over to the United States military for safekeeping. They were duly delivered, in the early 1950s, to Fort Knox in an elaborate operation code-named Klondike. The treasure was eventually returned to Hungary in 1978.

This would be just another story of political intrigue were it not for one strange fact: according to a memorandum in the State Department, the soldiers designated to guard the treasure were told that the boxes contained "the wings and engine of a flying saucer."

This type of misinformation may well have been common. "Is it effective?" asked researcher William Moore. "Certainly in the Klondike situation it was, because unsubstantiated stories about parts of a flying saucer being stored at Fort Knox continue to be part of the UFO crash/retrieval rumour mill to this very day. How many other similar rumours have a similar origin is anybody's guess."

The Spitzbergen Saucer That Wasn't:

For many years, tales have circulated to the effect that in the early 1950's a UFO crashed on the island of Spitzbergen, Norway, and, under circumstances similar to those that allegedly occurred at both Aztec and Roswell, was recovered along with its deceased alien crew.

On March 22, 1968, the State Department forwarded to a host of official bodies within the American intelligence community (including the CIA, the National Security Agency and Army Intelligence) a translation of a March 12, 1968 news article titled "Flying Saucers? They're A Myth!" that had been written by Viillen Lyustiberg, science editor of the Novosti Press Agency in Russia and that included a small mention of the Spitzbergen allegations.

The relevant section of the article stated:

"An abandoned silvery disc was found in the deep rock coal seams in Norwegian coal mines on Spitzbergen. It was pierced and marked by micrometeor impacts and bore all traces of having performed a long space voyage. It was sent for analysis to the Pentagon and disappeared there."

The CIA, Army, State Department and NSA have all declassified their files pertaining to their apparent interest in Soviet news articles on UFOs in general and the Spitzbergen event in particular.

However, the NSA's copy of the document differs significantly from those of its allied agencies. On the NSA's copy, someone had circled the specific section of the article that referred to the Spitzbergen crash with the word "PLANT."

This, again, would seem to suggest that this was a faked crashed UFO story, purposefully planted by persons currently unknown but known to the all-powerful National Security Agency.

Monkeys in the Desert?
And, finally, there is Kingman.

For years, interesting stories and accounts have circulated concerning the crash of a UFO at Kingman, Arizona in 1953 - and at the height of Operation Upshot-Knothole: a series of eleven nuclear test shots conducted over the border at the Nevada Test Site.

Perhaps a UFO really did crash at Kingman; however, I have uncovered files showing that in the same precise time-frame (and specifically as part of the Upshot-Knothole tests), the military was secretly test-flying drone aircraft in the area with monkeys on-board.

Might such a drone have crashed? Either by accident or design, was a crashed UFO story created to hide the security aspects of the affair?

While the image of an unmanned drone aircraft packed with a "crew" of monkeys flying across – and ultimately crashing in – the deserts of the southwest might sound laughable and bizarre in the extreme, official papers establishing that such tests were indeed undertaken have surfaced.

A document titled *Early Cloud Penetration*, dated January 27, 1956, and prepared by the Air Research and Development Command at Kirtland Air Force Base, New Mexico, states in part:

> "In the event of nuclear warfare the AF is confronted with two special problems. First is the hazard to flight crews who may be forced to fly through an atomic cloud. Second is the hazard to ground crews who maintain the aircraft after it has flown through the cloud...In the 1953 Upshot-Knothole tests, monkeys were used so that experiments could be conducted on larger animals nearer the size of man. QF-80 drone aircraft were used, their speed more nearly approximating that of current operational aircraft."

And that's just the 1940s and 1950s.

In the near future, I will do a follow-up post to this one that offers similar revelations pertaining to later, alleged UFO crashes.

You may disagree with me, and that is of course your right to do so. However, it seems to me that - for years - the crashed UFO community has been well and truly played, manipulated, and even controlled.

The trick to overcoming this is to throw out your belief systems and start fresh, with no preconceived ideas about crashed UFOs, and no emotion-driven need to believe in wrecked saucers, dead aliens, underground cryogenic chambers filled with ET body-parts, and all the rest.

Do that, be totally unbiased, and you may find some surprising facts about the origins of certain crashed UFO events.

Whether this will please you, dismay you, or cause you to throw out all your files and walk away from the subject remains to be seen, of course...

Conferences and Cultural Clashes 2010

Paranormal magazine's Richard Holland is someone who I've done a lot of work for, including full-length features and book-reviews. And then, in early 2010, there was this: a small, commentary-type piece from me on the differences – as I saw them, at least - between the conference scenes in Britain and the United States. *Conferences and Cultural Clashes* was its name:

'Oi, Nick! When are you going to get off your arse and write another *Bookend* for the magazine?' was the cheery, transatlantic e-question posed to me recently by *Paranormal's* editor, the good and fine Richard Holland. Well, okay, Richard didn't *quite* word it like that, but you get the picture.

But, I have to confess, it *has* been some time since my last such missive was published; and so we put our collective thinking-caps on and came up with an idea: taking into consideration the fact that, until my early-thirties, I had lived in jolly old England, but have made pistol-packing Dallas, Texas my home for the last ten years, what about something that would focus on the differences between the respective conference scenes in Britain and America?

I do, after all, speak at a *lot* of gigs on both sides of the Atlantic, and so I told Richard that I would see what I could come up with. And, I have to say, it wasn't difficult, at all. Aside from the undeniable fact that Britain and America are two nations divided by a common-language (as many have rightly said!), there is one big difference between Blighty-based events and those hosted in the Land of the Free (at least, it *was* that way before Dubya, Cheney and the Patriot Act reared their ugly heads).

At the vast majority of U.S.-based UFO events at which I speak, the organisers invariably want the lecturers to deliver presentations that adhere to the notion that the flying saucer puzzle that has dominated the world of the unexplained since 1947, has extraterrestrial origins.

Similarly, when I'm speaking at gigs of a specifically cryptozoological nature in the States, it's more often than not the case that people want to hear that Bigfoot is simply an unidentified, flesh-and-blood ape; or that the Loch Ness Monsters are surviving plesiosaurs.

I have, quite literally, seen some of the head-honchos in the world of conference-organising in America react with anger, disbelief, shock, and downright puzzlement and embarrassment when I bring up the possibility in my presentations that Bigfoot might actually be a Tulpa-style thought-form, and that the monsters of Loch Ness might be nothing stranger than giant-eels.

And, you would *not* believe (well, you might) the reaction that was generated when, at several States-side gigs in 2005 – and in the wake of the publication of my book, *Body Snatchers in the Desert* – I offered the theory that the notorious incident that occurred at Roswell, New Mexico in July 1947, had less to do with flesh-and-blood aliens, and much more to do with dark and dubious military experiments of a very home-grown nature. Such was the backlash you might have thought I had just admitted to eating a couple of cuddly little puppies for lunch!

But, in Britain, I see a very different situation. Here, I see, and speak to, audiences that don't seem to need to uphold particular ideas and belief-systems, but who seem far more inclined to accept – or to at least consider – some of the more esoteric and alternative views that pervade the world of the weird.

So, why should that be? Certainly, one reason is that the conference circuit in the U.S. is very much more commercialised than in Britain; and the fact is that in America people want to hear about bug-eyed aliens, *X-Files*-type conspiracies, and still-surviving dinosaurs – and, moreover, these topics admittedly bring in the punters in their droves.

Of course, that doesn't – and never will – stop me from expressing my more alternative views on such matters. But, it *does* mean that while I am often met with slightly frosty smiles in the States if I opine that the best way to see Bigfoot may be to invoke it via ancient rite and ritual, in Britain's it's far more likely to result in a genial chat over a pint or several at the post-gig party.

Contactees and the Absurdities of Ufology 2010

Skylaire Alfvegren is a California-based writer who I occasionally run into at gigs of a Fortean and/or ufological nature, who writes for the League of Western Fortean Intermediatists, and who invited me to submit an editorial for the LOWFI website in February 2010 – on the subject of those always-controversial Contactees and their long-haired space-friends:

You can write about anything you like, just as long as it has some kind of western U.S. angle," said Skylaire Alfvegren recently, when she invited me to pen a guest editorial for the *League of Western Fortean Intermediatists*. Well, given the nature of Skylaire's invitation, it wasn't difficult to come up with a subject-matter.

After all, as some of you may know, just a couple of months ago New Page Books published my most recent title: *Contactees – A History of Alien-Human Interaction*. And as just about anyone and everyone who has ever dared immerse themselves in the strange and twilight realm of all things of a long, blond-haired and space-brotherly nature will know, the West-Coast – and specifically California - is where most of the other-worldly action occurred.

After all, there were the "Four Georges": Adamski, the transplanted Pole, and surely the definitive Contactee, whose purported CA-based encounters with Orthon the E.T. in the early years of the 1950s helped make his *Flying Saucers Have Landed* book (co-written with Irishman Desmond Leslie) a mammoth-seller; Van Tassel, of both Giant Rock and Integratron fame; Hunt Williamson, who memorably contacted the Space Brothers via the medium of the Ouija board; and King, founder of the Aetherius Society, who ultimately wound up in California, after leaving behind his homeland of England.

And, of course, there was Orfeo Angelucci – a weak character whose life was dominated by ill health and anxiety. That is, until the early 1950s, when his Los Angeles-based encounters with the space-hippies elevated his mind and body to whole new levels and uncharted realms.

And who can forget Truman Bethurum? Certainly not me! Although Bethurum's infamous 1952 encounters with the hot and flirty Captain Aura Rhanes occurred on Mormon Mesa, Nevada, it was L.A. where Bethurum and his wife made their home – that is, at least, until the marriage collapsed after the gorgeous Aura succeeded in getting her cosmic claws into lucky old Truman.

In other words, it's pretty much impossible to have a discussion about the Contactees without bringing the West Coast firmly into the equation. Okay, moving on…

I'm often asked why – as someone who primarily digs into the issue of UFOs and governmental secrecy – I'm so interested in the stories of the West Coast Contactees. The answer is actually very simple: despite what the naysayers may loudly proclaim, that strange and surreal band of largely long-gone characters provides us with a deep insight into what really lies at the heart of the UFO puzzle that has for so long dazzled and dumbfounded us.

And here's what I mean by that:

One of the biggest problems that has long beset the Contactee movement is that the believers and the doubters rigidly insist (for the most part, at least) on looking at the phenomenon from

Giant Rock, Contactee Central.

purely black-and-white perspectives. For them, the claims of the Contactees are overwhelmingly bogus, or they must be accepted literally in the fashion the Contactees described them. Both groups, in my view, however, are totally missing the point.

Even the most cursory study of the Space Brother controversy makes it abundantly clear that far from being a mystery of just the last 60 years or so, in reality it's a very, very old phenomenon indeed, and one that has probably been with us ever since the first spark of intelligence popped into the brain of the most primitive of all proto-humans.

Vallee's *Passport to Magonia* and *Messengers of Deception*, Keel's *Operation Trojan Horse*, and the writings of Greg Bishop make that fact abundantly clear – providing one is willing to look beyond, and appreciate and understand, the carefully-created *Matrix*-style environment in which many of the encounters of the West Coast Contactees occurred.

George Adamski never met an alien named Orthon – and he never took wild flights around the solar system. Likewise, George Hunt Williamson's fascination with both the board and the planchette did not put him in contact with long-haired Venusians. And, as much as it saddens me to say so, there never was a Captain Aura Rhanes of the equally non-existent planet of Clarion.

But…those same Contactees did experience something…

And, it is that something which has utilised certain, key archetypes throughout history as a means to interact with those elements of the Human Race that it chooses (probably at random) to do its bidding, to spread the word, and to elevate both our consciousness and our world-view.

Centuries ago it appeared in the form of gods, angels, demons, fairies and goblins. Sixty years ago, the phenomenon reawakened from its slumber, headed for the heart of California, and mind-fucked dozens of souls with its messages of peace, love and cosmic harmony.

Today, it appears in the form of ugly, black-eyed dwarfs who have an apparent fascination with human reproduction, the ecological collapse of the planet, and anal probes.

One hundred years from now, that same something will most assuredly still be playing its games on the West Coast and just about everywhere else, too. But, by then, the Grays and the long-haired ones will be nothing but distant memories, and in their place will be time-travellers, inter-dimensional pixies, or something else of an equally spaced-out nature. The message, however – as well as the profound change that the experience causes in those who are exposed to it – will remain.

And, there's one other matter, too: the Contactees of the West-Coast were fun. They were characters. They were the sort of people with whom you could hang out, drink a few cold beers, and have a good time. But, today's Ufology has lost much of that fun and innocence.

I speak at a lot of conferences, and over the last couple of years or so, I have seen a trend that began a decade or more ago now increasing on a significant scale. It's the move to make the UFO movement a very serious one – A VERY SERIOUS ONE.

I occasionally get criticized because I like to speak to audiences in a relaxed fashion – and, for me, that usually means in a black t-shirt and black jeans. So what? As the Contactees noted, it's the message that matters, right? Not whether "Researcher A" wears a suit, or I wear a *Rammstein* t-shirt. Well, to some, it does matter – and increasingly so.

But, frankly, I am tired of seeing nicely ironed black suits, crisp, white shirts and bright red ties on-stage. I'm tired of the carefully-delivered phrases that are punctuated by perfectly-timed pauses – to allow the audience to clap wildly, as if the lecturer in question is running for a place in the fucking Oval Office. And, I'm tired of the grim, overly-serious faces that so many of these humourless souls wear. You know the faces I mean: they're the ones usually reserved for Taser-wielding cops and airport security officials.

Like it or not, the UFO mystery is full of absurdities – whether it's the aforementioned anal probes; ET's obsession with collecting soil samples, seemingly ad infinitum; Joe Simonton's cosmic pancakes; the aliens' love of Strawberry ice cream (frankly, I'd like to know what's wrong with chocolate ice cream?) and crappy Tibetan music; and… well, the list goes on and on.

The West-Coast Contactees recognized – as have many of us that have delved deep into their stories – that absurdity and Ufology go together hand-in-glove. We should not try and force the UFO issue into some sort of dour, political movement. Nor should we ignore the stories – such as those of the Contactees – that some researchers deem unworthy of study, or that are viewed as embarrasments to the VERY SERIOUS NATURE of the phenomenon that they are trying to force on us.

Of course, there is a serious nature to the UFO issue – but politicising Ufology, and making it (yep, it's time for capital letters again) VERY SERIOUS doesn't help solve the riddle of what's afoot. All it does is make those same VERY SERIOUS ufologists feel good at a personal level. Indeed, it's a feel-good factor that, in their minds, brings them closer to Woodward and Bernstein than it does to the tinfoil hat brigade, or to the little old ladies who donate their life-savings to help fund some non-existent Martian mission on Earth.

But, regardless of what you, me or anyone else thinks about the stories and the claims of the West Coast Contactees, their refreshing attitude of not really giving a shit about what the rest of the UFO field – or the general public and the media - thought about them, is something from which many people in today's Ufology can learn a great deal.

The stories of the Contactees were interesting and absurd. Ufology is interesting and absurd. Those of us within Ufology are interesting and absurd (albeit in varying degrees!). The Contactees knew this and they embraced it – and, as a result and in the process, they attracted audiences of 12,000 out at Giant Rock, California.

Today's VERY SERIOUS suit-and-tie brigade generally achieves audiences of a couple of hundred at most – despite their political style, and their on-stage rallying – at even the most widely publicised UFO gigs; many of which actually result in the organiser(s) losing money as a result of the lack of public interest and support.

Methinks everyone in Ufology can learn something from that.

The Roswell UFO Museum.

Why Roswell Will Never Be Solved 2010

Roswell continues to plague and annoy me immensely to this very day – largely due to the near-mythical status that has been wrongly afforded the affair; as this post – that I prepared in early 2010 for Rich Reynolds's *The UFO Iconoclast(s)* – acutely demonstrates. But, more than anything else, the article demonstrates why, in my humble opinion, we'll never really get our hands upon the hard evidence of what actually happened at Roswell. This is actually a good thing for the ufological true-believers – because, if Roswell *did* have a *non*-extraterrestrial point of origin (as I believe to be the case), then evidence of such would ensure that the whole vile house-of-cards would collapse in on itself. So, in many respects, it works in the favour of the true-believer (which I no longer am) for Roswell to be ever-shrouded in mystery. Maybe you'll agree with me or not, but here are my views on the whole, sorry affair, *Why Roswell Will Never Be Solved*:

With a blog-post title like that, you might think I have given up the hunt, lost my enthusiasm, or taken on a decidedly pessimistic approach to Roswell. I would, however, strongly disagree. Rather, my words are borne out of what I would say is a realistic and practical approach to the Roswell debate - or, perhaps, the Roswell problem is a better term.

And here's why I am certain that Roswell will never be resolved.

Unless you include whistle-blower documentation such as the MJ12 documents as being evidence in support of what happened - or did not happen - on the Foster Ranch, Lincoln County,

New Mexico on the fateful day in early July 1947, the only real data of any significance that we have in-hand comes from the witnesses.

And that's a good thing; a very good thing. The reason being that without the reports, testimony and recollections of the witnesses, all we would have would be a couple of pages of official documents (such as a 1-page FBI memo and a few other scant items), a handful of press-photographs, and a bunch of newspaper clippings. In other words, whatever happened at Roswell, it is thanks to the witnesses that we know something of significance occurred.

So, witness testimony is massively important and has taken us to where we are today with respect to Roswell - which, unfortunately, is a confusing, hall-of-mirrors realm inhabited by tales of crashed UFOs, dead aliens, crash-test-dummies, Mogul-balloons, weather-balloons, flying-wings, Nazi-saucers, Japanese PoWs, Unit 731, V-2 rockets, atomic mishaps, and more. In other words, the witness testimony and second-hand and third-hand testimony is huge - but, rather than uniformly presenting one version of events, the testimony and data has merely muddied the waters even further.

And there's another problem, and it's a big one; a very big one, in fact. Due to the passage of time and the inevitability of death, most of the witnesses are gone. Ten or fifteen years from now they will likely all be gone.

Then, with our (thus far) one and only meaningful source of data gone forever, how will we take Roswell further? How will we solve Roswell? Will we even be able to solve Roswell - ever? That's where I take issue with those who desperately want Roswell to be proved extraterrestrial before they, too, go to the big Hangar 18 in the sky, and who earnestly believe it will be solved, to the point where we have hard evidence, not just a body of intriguing, interesting and notable testimony.

Here's the problem that many fail to deal with in a level-headed fashion: witness testimony is vital to any investigation and can shed welcome light (sometimes a little light and sometimes a great deal of light) on matters of profound controversy - which Roswell most assuredly is. The problem, however, is that no matter how much testimony and witness material we get, that will still never, ever, definitively prove what happened at Roswell.

The reason the Roswell debate is ongoing - despite literally hundreds of people having offered testimony in varying degrees (first-hand, second-hand, third-hand, etc.) is because no-one has thus far delivered the goods. And by the goods, I mean, of course, a body, a body-part, undeniable extraterrestrial wreckage, or undeniable "Roswell UFO Files" that can be proved to have originated with one or more elements of the official world back in the late-1940s.

So, by 2025, when the Roswell research community will have likely lost its strongest and only source of quality data - the people and the witnesses - the only way we can ever hope to solve Roswell is by getting access to the bodies, the craft and the documentation - if such even exist.

So, let's go there:

THE DOCUMENTS:
If the device that came down on the Foster Ranch really was a weather-balloon, then the chances are that the amount of paperwork generated on the affair might have been so small that it will never surface - precisely because there's barely anything to see that we don't have already.

Similarly, if the Roswell craft was a Mogul Balloon, then, it seems that, from reading the USAF's report of 1994, documentation on the crash was never generated to any meaningful degree in the first place. And, if Roswell involved Japanese prisoners-of-war, as detailed in my *Body Snatchers in the Desert* book, well...everyone I spoke with said that because these were supposedly semi-illegal experiments (borne out of the human radiation experiments of the 1940s and 1950s - for which the official Government report on the 40s/50s experiments confirms countless files were destroyed years ago), all the files were destroyed to protect the guilty.

So, in other words, logic dictates that substantial and significant paperwork would only exist if the Roswell event involved a crashed alien craft and bodies (or something else that was equally-weirdly Fortean or anomalous). But, the irony is that if E.T. really did crash on the Foster Ranch, then it is this paperwork more than any other that the Government will never, ever, let us see.

Consider the facts as we know them: the USAF checked, checked and checked again and found no paper-trail on Roswell (aside from a couple of pages, such as the already-known 1-page FBI document of July 1947), as did all of the other agencies approached. The General Accounting Office could not find anything, and neither could Congressman Steven Schiff

Now, if the USAF's Mogul and crash-test dummy stories are indeed cover-stories (and not genuine attempts to put Roswell to rest), for the Air Force to lie to the GAO, and to lie to Schiff would suggest that any theoretical "Roswell Files" have to be buried so incredibly deep, and the USAF must be supremely confident (to lie on such a huge and widespread scale) that those files will never surface and cannot be accessed by anyone who isn't clued-in on what really happened. But if that is so, then how do we get the files?

FOIA hasn't worked at all; Schiff couldn't do it; and the GAO got absolutely nowhere. So, this is a question I'd genuinely be interested in seeing people answer: in view of those points directly above in this paragraph, when the witnesses are all dead and we can only then go after the files, how will we get access to them? And Disclosure doesn't stand a chance in hell of working. So, if we can't get the documents, what next? That just leaves the bodies and the craft.

THE BODIES:
If the accounts of alien-bodies at Roswell were borne out of crash-test-dummy experiments, they wouldn't have been saved and stored in some secret hangar - that would be a totally insane scenario.

If they were Japanese: well, I was told that because the high-altitude experiments were failures, there was no reason to preserve the bodies. And again, that's totally logical: preserving for decades a bunch of mangled Japanese bodies would be manifestly absurd, because to do so would serve no purpose at all. Indeed, the only possible reason why any potential bodies would be preserved and saved would be if they were alien in origin - or were, again, of some other weird, Fortean origin.

But, ironically, just like the paperwork, if bodies were found on, or near, the Foster Ranch, and they were alien, then they too would have to be buried so deep (perhaps literally!) that we can't get to them.

And, remember: if the bodies were alien and were preserved, and still are preserved somewhere today, that place (such as a real-life equivalent of the mythical Hangar 18) would have to be a secure, sterile facility, where the corpses would require storage in the best preservation situation as possible. In other words, probably somewhere underground, in tightly-sealed canisters.

So, just with the paperwork: if Roswell involved aliens, then how do we access, photograph or steal alien bodies stored 50-feet underground, that are preserved in sealed containers and are no doubt heavily guarded?

The answer is simple: we can't.

So, we move onto number 3:

THE CRAFT:

As with the bodies, access to any Roswell craft of alien origins would be impossible to anyone outside of what would undoubtedly be a tightly-knit circle of people in-the-know. So, here's where we are currently at with Roswell: nearly everyone involved is dead. Fifteen years from now they will likely all be gone - and, to date, that's our only significant source of data on Roswell. And, I just don't see (because of the reasons outlined above) how we can gain access to the documents, the bodies and the craft - if they exist.

Now before people get all emotional and defensive, bear in mind that my approach to the Roswell problem is not a defeatist or a pessimistic one. Rather, it's a realistic approach to the problem of solving Roswell. And by solving I do mean solving; not just gathering more testimony. Testimony can be great. But testimony is not proof. And we need proof, if we are to take Roswell to the next level.

I would be genuinely interested to hear how people think Roswell can be taken any further than it is now, when the witnesses are all gone and everything else, such as paperwork, bodies and materials (if it exists, of course) are all hidden far from prying eyes.

Unless the Government decides to release anything of an E.T. nature relative to Roswell, the fact is that we are very close to where Roswell will not be able to be taken any further, and we will be going around in circles; as, in many ways, we are already.

For example, you only have to check out some of the on-line debates about whether there were four bodies or five bodies recovered. Or: whether or not a Mogul balloon was big enough to create the debris field at the Foster Ranch. These debates go on for days; sometimes they go on for weeks. Fucking weeks! But, those debates can never, ever resolve anything. All they can do is offer possibilities that this person is right, or that person is wrong.

I think it's very likely that 50 years from now, people (if they're still even interested in Roswell - which they may very well not be) will still be debating the size of the debris field at the Foster Ranch; or why Marcel Sr. didn't show Marcel Jr. the memory-metal; or why the USAF has changed its story on Roswell several times.

And, don't get me wrong: these are all highly important questions. But the reason we'll be forever doomed to asking them is because, unless the Government changes its stance, we stand zero chance of getting to the hard data that could solve Roswell.

That's not defeatist: it's realistic. The head-in-the-clouds approach of vainly hoping we'll all live to see Roswell resolved will solve nothing.

Now, with that all said, could there be an alternative to getting the answer and, ultimately, the proof? Well, the only thing I can remotely think of is if some old man or woman has at their home an Aladdin's Cave of aged and fading documentation that they illegally obtained before the lid clamped down on Roswell, and who are waiting for the right person to present it to come along?

Could such a thing happen? You'd damn well better hope it does.

Because, if it doesn't, there's absolutely no denying that Roswell will finally join all those other never-to-be-firmly-solved-and-proved mysteries that include (a) who killed JFK?; and (b) who was Jack the Ripper?

Behold, the Cardiff Giant!

The Strange Tale of the Cardiff Giant 2010

It's perhaps fitting that I close this book with an article from my regular *Letter from America* column that appears within the pages of each and every issue of the Centre for Fortean Zoology's in-house publication, *Animals & Men*. This one, from 2010, tells the truly strange story of the Cardiff Giant:

The tale of the legendary Cardiff Giant is just about as weird, as surreal, and as convoluted as any tale can possibly get! And, without doubt, it was one of the most infamous and audacious hoaxes in American history.

Essentially, the giant was nothing less than a 10-foot-tall purported "petrified man," said to have been uncovered on October 16, 1869 by workmen engaged in digging a well behind the barn of one William C. "Stub" Newell in Cardiff, New York.

In reality, however, the giant was nothing of the sort. It was actually the creation of a New York tobacconist named George Hull; an atheist, who decided to create the mighty-form after a heated argument with a fundamentalist minister – a certain Mr. Turk - about the passage in *Genesis 6:4* to the effect that giants once roamed the Earth.

Hull's master-plan very quickly came to overwhelming fruition: he secretly hired a group of men to carve the enormous man out of a block of gypsum in Fort Dodge, Iowa, telling them it was intended to be used in the creation of a monument to Abraham Lincoln that would stand proudly in the heart of New York City. When work was complete, Hull shipped the block to Chicago, where he hired a German stone-cutter to further carve it into the likeness of a man – not forgetting, in the process, to swear him to absolute secrecy.

The ruse was a highly ingenious one: a whole variety of stains and acids were used to make the giant appear both ancient and weathered. In addition, the giant's surface was beaten with steel knitting-needles embedded in a board. The purpose: to simulate pores on the skin. If nothing else, Hull had carefully and skillfully thought out his grand-plan.

Then, in November 1868, Hull transported the giant by rail to the farm of his cousin, William Newell. No less than $2,600 was spent on the hoax in total – which was a sizeable amount of money, indeed, way back in the 1860s.

Almost twelve months later, Newell hired Gideon Emmons and Henry Nichols, ostensibly to dig a well, and on October 16, 1869, lo and behold they "found" the Cardiff Giant. One of the men reportedly exclaimed, in excited and exaggerated tones: "I declare: some old Indian has been buried here!"

But that was only the start of the matter: Newell quickly set up a tent over the giant and charged 25-cents for anyone and everyone who wanted to see it. Two days later, very pleased by the huge number of people who turned out to view the Cardiff Giant, he increased the price to 50 cents. Enterprise was truly the name of the game.

Archaeological scholars quickly pronounced the giant nothing more than a fake; while a number of geologists noticed there was no logical reason for digging a well in the exact spot the giant had been found. And Yale palaeontologist Othniel C. Marsh came right to the point, famously declaring the Cardiff Giant a "most decided humbug". There were, however, some gullible Christian fundamentalists and preachers who defended its legitimacy.

Ultimately, Hull sold his part-interest for the very impressive sum of $37,500 to a syndicate of five men headed by one David Hannum. They, then, clandestinely moved the giant form to Syracuse, New York for exhibition. Unsurprisingly, the giant drew such massive crowds that the famous showman P.T. Barnum offered $60,000 for a three-month lease of the giant. When the syndicate flatly turned him down, however, the always-resourceful and industrious Barnum hired a man to create a plaster replica – which quickly went on display in New York, amid claims that this was the real thing, and that the Cardiff Giant was the hoax!

As newspaper journalists gleefully reported on Barnum's version of the story, David Hannum was quoted as saying, "There's a sucker born every minute;" in reference to spectators paying to see Barnum's giant. Over time, the quotation was misattributed to P.T. Barnum himself. Hannum then tried to sue Barnum. In somewhat humorous fashion, however, the judge told Hannum to get his giant to swear on his own genuineness in court if he wanted an injunction in his favour. That was a tough one to achieve.

But still matters were not over: on December 10, Hull confessed the truth to the press. Then, on February 2, 1870 both giants were revealed as fakes in court, and the judge ruled that Barnum could not be sued for calling a fake giant a fake. And that was the end of the lawsuit, not surprisingly.

And the events stirred up something else too: they encouraged others to come forward with their very own versions of the Cardiff Giant. As evidence of this, in 1876 the "Solid Muldoon" surfaced out of Beulah, Colorado and was exhibited at 50 cents a ticket. There was also a rumour going around that Barnum had offered to buy it for $20,000. It was, needless to say, a fake – and possibly one that George Hull himself had a hand in.

One year later, in 1877, the owner of Taughannock House hotel on Cayuga Lake, New York, hired his own merry band of men to create a fake petrified man, and who carefully placed it precisely where the workers that were expanding the hotel would eventually find it. Once again, publicity and public interest were impressive. But, it was still a hoax.

Then, in 1892, a certain Jefferson "Soapy" Smith, the de facto ruler of the town of Creede, Colorado, bought a petrified man – "McGinty," as he became known - for $3,000 and exhibited it for 10 cents a look. Interestingly, this giant was actually real. That's right: a human-body, deliberately injected with chemicals for preservation. Soapy enthusiastically displayed McGinty from 1892 to 1895 throughout Colorado and the northwest United States.

Seven years on – 1899, to be precise - a petrified man was said to have been found in Fort Benton, Montana. The body was supposedly identified as that of U.S. Civil War General Thomas Francis Meagher. Meagher had drowned in the Missouri River two years previously. The petrified man was transported to New York for exhibition; but, needless to say, it was not the general, at all.

The Cardiff Giant – which started all the fuss – continued to surface from time to time. However, its place in the limelight was clearly waning. In 1901 the giant appeared on display at the Pan-American Exposition, but failed to generate any significant attention or publicity.

Then, some years later, an Iowa-based publisher purchased it – for use as a coffee-table, no less! Seemingly eventually growing tired of the giant, in 1947 the man sold it to the Farmers' Museum in Cooperstown, New York, where it is still on display.

And there's another very good reason why the controversy of the Cardiff Giant refuses to roll over and die.

In January 2010, I gave a lecture at Cooperstown – as part of the *Ghosts of Cooperstown* event that included presentations from the people behind the History Channel's *Ghost Hunters* series – on the subject of one of my deep passions: cryyptozoology; which is the search for unknown animals, such as Bigfoot, the Loch Ness Monster and the Chupacabras.

After the lecture, a local woman named Sally came up to me and swore that her father had seen the Cardiff Giant striding through the woods of Cooperstown late one winter's night in 2007. I asked Sally if she was joking. She was not. Her father, Sally said, had been driving home at around 11.00 p.m. one Friday night – after visiting friends in Albany, NY.

As Sally's father approached one particular stretch of road enveloped by trees, he was shocked to the core by the sight of the Cardiff Giant looming out of the woods and striding across the road in several mighty steps. Not surprisingly, he hit the brakes.

Sally told me both she and her father, as locals, had been to see the Cardiff Giant on display at the local museum on several occasions over the years. They also knew full well that it was nothing more than a century-old hoax. So, how could a hoaxed creation be seen wandering the chilled woods of Cooperstown in 2007?

Sally's opinion was that the Cardiff Giant that her father saw was not the same entity that currently rests in the Farmer's Museum. Rather, she felt, he had been blessed with a sighting of a thought-form – a Tulpa – that had been conjured into existence by the sheer unconscious will of those who wished to believe it was real. It was a mind-monster, in other words – one that cannot exist unless people believe in it.

Could it really be the case that a mind-originated Cardiff Giant haunts the darkened parts of Cooperstown, one destined to roam the neighborhood by night, until such a time that a lack of belief in its existence dooms it to inevitable annihilation?

It was as good a theory as any, I suggested. And, as someone who has dug deeply into the world of thought-forms and Tulpas, I reasoned it made a great deal of sense, too.

The saga of the Cardiff Giant, I suspect, is far from over…

***

Afterword

And while the mystery of the Cardiff Giant looks set to continue, this book does not! Here, now, ends the varied selection of my written output spanning 1982 to 2010. I hope it entertained, informed, and intrigued you. For me, it brought back a lot of memories as I dug into my old files, and spent days searching for old CDs containing equally old Word documents from years past and lands now far-away (Blighty, in other words). Perhaps in another 28 years (when I'll be 73 – what a terrifying thought!) I'll get around to doing *Volume II*. Until then, adios…!

About Nick Redfern

Nick Redfern works full-time as an author, lecturer and journalist. He writes about a wide range of unsolved mysteries, including Bigfoot, UFOs, the Loch Ness Monster, alien encounters, and government conspiracies. Nick writes regularly for *UFO Magazine*; *Fate*; *TAPS Paramagazine*; and *Fortean Times*. His previous books include *Man-Monkey*; *Monsters of Texas* (with Ken Gerhard); *The NASA Conspiracies*; *Contactees*; and *Memoirs of a Monster Hunter*. Nick has appeared on numerous television shows, including VH1's *Legend Hunters*; the BBC's *Out of this World*; History Channel's *Monster Quest* and *UFO Hunters*; National Geographic Channel's *Paranatural*; and SyFy Channel's *Proof Positive*. He is the co-host, with Raven Meindel, of the popular, weekly radio-show, *Exploring All Realms*. Nick lives in Arlington, Texas with his wife, Dana.

THE ACKNOWLEDGMENTS:

I would like to express my sincere thanks to all the magazines and newspapers that were kind enough to give their permission for the aforementioned articles, reviews and items to appear in the pages of this book. Particular thanks must go to Mike Lockley of the *Chase Post*; Phyllis Galde of *Fate*; Rich Reynolds of *The UFO Iconoclast(s)*; and the *Daily Express*. I would also like to thank my good friend, and editor of *Space Girl Dead on Spaghetti Junction*, Jon Downes, for encouraging me to put the book together, and for his hard work on bringing it to fruition. Cheers, matey!

THE WORLD'S WEIRDEST PUBLISHING COMPANY

HOW TO START A PUBLISHING EMPIRE

Unlike most mainstream publishers, we have a non-commercial remit, and our mission statement claims that "we publish books because they deserve to be published, not because we think that we can make money out of them". Our motto is the Latin Tag *Pro bona causa facimus* (we do it for good reason), a slogan taken from a children's book *The Case of the Silver Egg* by the late Desmond Skirrow.

WIKIPEDIA: "The first book published was in 1988. *Take this Brother may it Serve you Well* was a guide to *Beatles* bootlegs by Jonathan Downes. It sold quite well, but was hampered by very poor production values, being photocopied, and held together by a plastic clip binder. In 1988 A5 clip binders were hard to get hold of, so the publishers took A4 binders and cut them in half with a hacksaw. It now reaches surprisingly high prices second hand.

The production quality improved slightly over the years, and after 1999 all the books produced were ringbound with laminated colour covers. In 2004, however, they signed an agreement with Lightning Source, and all books are now produced perfect bound, with full colour covers."

Until 2010 all our books, the majority of which are/were on the subject of mystery animals and allied disciplines, were published by `CFZ Press`, the publishing arm of the Centre for Fortean Zoology (CFZ), and we urged our readers and followers to draw a discreet veil over the books that we published that were completely off topic to the CFZ.

However, in 2010 we decided that enough was enough and launched a second imprint, `Fortean Words` which aims to cover a wide range of non animal-related esoteric subjects. Other imprints will be launched as and when we feel like it, however the basic ethos of the company remains the same: Our job is to publish books and magazines that we feel are worth publishing, whether or not they are going to sell. Money is, after all - as my dear old Mama once told me - a rather vulgar subject, and she would be rolling in her grave if she thought that her eldest son was somehow in `trade`.

Luckily, so far our tastes have turned out not to be that rarified after all, and we have sold far more books than anyone ever thought that we would, so there is a moral in there somewhere...

Jon Downes,
Woolsery, North Devon
July 2010

Other Books in Print

CFZ Yearbook 2011 edited by Jonathan Downes
Karl Shuker's Alien Zoo by Shuker, Dr Karl P.N
Tetrapod Zoology Book One by Naish, Dr Darren
The Mystery Animals of Ireland by Gary Cunningham and Ronan Coghlan
Monsters of Texas by Gerhard, Ken
The Great Yokai Encyclopaedia by Freeman, Richard
NEW HORIZONS: Animals & Men *issues 16-20 Collected Editions Vol. 4* by Downes, Jonathan
A Daintree Diary -
Tales from Travels to the Daintree Rainforest in tropical north Queensland, Australia by Portman, Carl
Strangely Strange but Oddly Normal by Roberts, Andy
Centre for Fortean Zoology Yearbook 2010 by Downes, Jonathan
Predator Deathmatch by Molloy, Nick
Star Steeds and other Dreams by Shuker, Karl
CHINA: A Yellow Peril? by Muirhead, Richard
Mystery Animals of the British Isles: The Western Isles by Vaudrey, Glen
Giant Snakes - Unravelling the coils of mystery by Newton, Michael
Mystery Animals of the British Isles: Kent by Arnold, Neil
Centre for Fortean Zoology Yearbook 2009 by Downes, Jonathan
CFZ EXPEDITION REPORT: Russia 2008 by Richard Freeman *et al*, Shuker, Karl (fwd)
Dinosaurs and other Prehistoric Animals on Stamps - A Worldwide catalogue by Shuker, Karl P. N
Dr Shuker's Casebook by Shuker, Karl P.N
The Island of Paradise - chupacabra UFO crash retrievals,
and accelerated evolution on the island of Puerto Rico by Downes, Jonathan
The Mystery Animals of the British Isles: Northumberland and Tyneside by Hallowell, Michael J
Centre for Fortean Zoology Yearbook 1997 by Downes, Jonathan (Ed)
Centre for Fortean Zoology Yearbook 2002 by Downes, Jonathan (Ed)
Centre for Fortean Zoology Yearbook 2000/1 by Downes, Jonathan (Ed)
Centre for Fortean Zoology Yearbook 1998 by Downes, Jonathan (Ed)
Centre for Fortean Zoology Yearbook 2003 by Downes, Jonathan (Ed)

In the wake of Bernard Heuvelmans by Woodley, Michael A
CFZ EXPEDITION REPORT: Guyana 2007 by Richard Freeman *et al*, Shuker, Karl (fwd)
Centre for Fortean Zoology Yearbook 1999 by Downes, Jonathan (Ed)
Big Cats in Britain Yearbook 2008 by Fraser, Mark (Ed)
Centre for Fortean Zoology Yearbook 1996 by Downes, Jonathan (Ed)
THE CALL OF THE WILD - Animals & Men issues 11-15 Collected Editions Vol. 3 by Downes, Jonathan (ed)
Ethna's Journal by Downes, C N
Centre for Fortean Zoology Yearbook 2008 by Downes, J (Ed)
DARK DORSET -Calendar Custome by Newland, Robert J
Extraordinary Animals Revisited by Shuker, Karl
MAN-MONKEY - In Search of the British Bigfoot by Redfern, Nick
Dark Dorset Tales of Mystery, Wonder and Terror by Newland, Robert J and Mark North
Big Cats Loose in Britain by Matthews, Marcus
MONSTER! - The A-Z of Zooform Phenomena by Arnold, Neil
The Centre for Fortean Zoology 2004 Yearbook by Downes, Jonathan (Ed)
The Centre for Fortean Zoology 2007 Yearbook by Downes, Jonathan (Ed)
CAT FLAPS! Northern Mystery Cats by Roberts, Andy
Big Cats in Britain Yearbook 2007 by Fraser, Mark (Ed)
BIG BIRD! - Modern sightings of Flying Monsters by Gerhard, Ken
THE NUMBER OF THE BEAST - Animals & Men issues 6-10 Collected Editions Vol. 1 by Downes, Jonathan (Ed)
IN THE BEGINNING - Animals & Men issues 1-5 Collected Editions Vol. 1 by Downes, Jonathan
STRENGTH THROUGH KOI - They saved Hitler's Koi and other stories by Downes, Jonathan
The Smaller Mystery Carnivores of the Westcountry by Downes, Jonathan
CFZ EXPEDITION REPORT: Gambia 2006 by Richard Freeman *et al*, Shuker, Karl (fwd)
The Owlman and Others by Jonathan Downes
The Blackdown Mystery by Downes, Jonathan
Big Cats in Britain Yearbook 2006 by Fraser, Mark (Ed)
Fragrant Harbours - Distant Rivers by Downes, John T
Only Fools and Goatsuckers by Downes, Jonathan
Monster of the Mere by Jonathan Downes
Dragons:More than a Myth by Freeman, Richard Alan
Granfer's Bible Stories by Downes, John Tweddell
Monster Hunter by Downes, Jonathan

Fortean Words

The Centre for Fortean Zoology has for several years led the field in Fortean publishing. CFZ Press is the only publishing company specialising in books on monsters and mystery animals. CFZ Press has published more books on this subject than any other company in history and has attracted such well known authors as Andy Roberts, Nick Redfern, Michael Newton, Dr Karl Shuker, Neil Arnold, Dr Darren Naish, Jon Downes, Ken Gerhard and Richard Freeman.

Now CFZ Press are launching a new imprint. Fortean Words is a new line of books dealing with Fortean subjects other than cryptozoology, which is - after all - the subject the CFZ are best known for. Fortean Words is being launched with a spectacular multi-volume series called *Haunted Skies* which covers British UFO sightings between 1940 and 2010. Former policeman John Hanson and his long-suffering partner Dawn Holloway have compiled a peerless library of sighting reports, many that have been not made public before.

Other forthcoming books include a look at the Berwyn Mountains UFO case by renowned Fortean Andy Roberts and a series of books by transatlantic researcher Nick Redfern.

CFZ Press are dedicated to maintaining the fine quality of their works with Fortean Words. New authors tackling new subjects will always be encouraged, and we hope that our books will continue to be as ground breaking and popular as ever.

www.ingramcontent.com/pod-product-compliance
Ingram Content Group UK Ltd.
Pitfield, Milton Keynes, MK11 3LW, UK
UKHW021319180426
11947UKWH00015B/1323